How To Do
Civil War
Research

How To Do
Civil War
Research

Richard A. Sauers, Ph.D.

Combined Publishing
Pennsylvania

PUBLISHER'S NOTE

The headquarters of Combined Publishing are located midway between Valley Forge and the Germantown battlefield, on the outskirts of Philadelphia. From its beginnings, our company has been steeped in the oldest traditions of American history and publishing. Our historic surroundings help maintain our focus on   history and our books strive to uphold the standards of style, quality and durability first established by the earliest bookmakers of Germantown and Philadelphia so many years ago. Our famous monk-and-console logo reflects our commitment to the modern and yet historic enterprise of publishing.

We call ourselves Combined Publishing because we have always felt that our goals could only be achieved through a "combined" effort by authors, publishers and readers. We have always tried to maintain maximum communication between these three key players in the reading experience.

We are always interested in hearing from prospective authors about new books in our field. We also like to hear from our readers and invite you to contact us at our offices in Pennsylvania with any questions, comments or suggestions, or if you have difficulty finding our books at a local bookseller.

For information, address:
Combined Publishing
P.O. Box 307
Conshohocken, PA 19428
E-mail: combined@combinedpublishing.com
Web: www.combinedpublishing.com
Orders: 1-800-418-6065

Revised Edition Copyright © 2000 by Richard A. Sauers
This is a revised edition of a book previously published as *Research Secrets of a Civil War Historian*.
Original Copyright© 1995

Cataloging-in-Publication Data available from the Library of Congress

ISBN 1-58097-041-9 (pb)

Printed in the United States of America.

Contents

Introduction

As a Civil War historian who has researched many, many topics and who has assisted in several research endeavors, I am often asked questions on how to research topics, from determining what information is needed, to where and how to find this information, to obtaining permission to publish and the actual publishing process itself.

This guide is ideal for both the beginning researcher who has discovered an interest in the Civil War, as well as researchers who are more advanced. People researching ancestors, Civil War soldiers, regiments, battles, collectibles, and many other topics will also find this guide to be a tremendous help. Lastly, those of you who already have experience in this field will find helpful pointers and suggestions, especially about manuscript collections, repositories, libraries, and archives.

Doing research can be extremely rewarding. There is the thrill of finding information or images very few people may have seen, of forgotten documents and "lost" treasures, of finding letters written by an ancestor, or of records from a regiment in which you are interested. You will learn some new skills and improve on other skills you already possess. This guide will help make your research easier, more efficient, and more productive. Now let's get down to business.

This book is organized following the six easy steps to Civil War research:

1. Focusing
2. Setting out on your journey
3. Finding the information you need
4. Organizing your information
5. Writing

Focusing

The very first thing you need to do is define what you are searching for. For instance, if it is information on your great grandfather and his regiment in the Civil War, define it as:

Captain James Merrill Linn, Company H,

51st Pennsylvania Volunteer Infantry.

Include all data you already know—you might have to start with just a name and then try to find the man's rank and regiment.

Or you may have purchased a photograph from the period and wish to identify the person.

Or you have found a sword identified as belonging to Captain Linn and want to find out more about the man, the duties of his rank, his activities during the war, and the battles in which he was involved. This type of information is important for your own use, as well as for documentation and authentication of artifacts.

The more information you find, the more interesting the story becomes, the more questions you will want to find answers to, leads you will want to follow, and the more you will contribute to what is known about this special period of time in our country's history.

But you must start with whatever data you already know, even if it's just the name of a person or a regiment. As we go through this book, you'll learn more about how to locate the missing pieces of data. The most important things you will need on your search are **patience, persistence, networking, and organization.**

★ **Patience.** Research can take a lot of time, and answers that are not readily available *can* often be found if you go through each step, one step at a time. Sometimes, like a puzzle, there will be missing pieces and by luck, serendipity, chance, or fate, the information or a clue will come to you. It is not uncommon for clues to come to you in your sleep; remember how when you are talking to someone, you can't seem to recall a name, although it's "just on the tip of your tongue" and you decide to forget it and a couple of hours later it just "pops" into your head? Well the same thing can happen with research. Be patient.

★ **Persistence.** Sometimes you will trace the data to a private collection to which you have no access. Talk to the owner or curator of the collection and explain what you are working on and what you need from him, such as permission to look at a diary, relic, or photograph.

This process can take time, so be patient, persistent, and maintain a friendly attitude. You want to be professional in your dealings with people so that others may also have access to these collections, and so that you will get to see the information you need. Some people are very proud of their holdings, and their homes are like small museums; other people are very guarded and secretive, wary of strangers, and suspicious of your motives. Give them time to get to know you. One possible suggestion is to meet them somewhere neutral for lunch, to discuss your research and let the person get to know you.

Give it time, go slow, and keep trying. If it gets completely hopeless and they've slammed a door in your face (figuratively or literally), move on to Networking, and try to find another way to get the same data.

★ **Networking.** This is an excellent way to find out where to look for information, to find out who has what material, to find other people who are interested in the same topic and who may be willing to share their data with you. A good place to start is with fellow Civil War buffs with whom you are friends, or who are in your Civil War Roundtable (CWRT) discussion group (see page 24). The Internet is also a great way to network with people from all over the world.

Ask librarians for their input; if they don't have the answer, ask if they know anyone else who might. Keep plugging away; the more people you ask, the better your chances of finding the person or library you need to get the data you want.

If you are totally stumped, you may need to pay an experienced researcher for help. This is where defining what you need can really help save time and money, since most researchers charge an hourly rate. One example is the National Archives. If you are unable to go there to do research, the Archives staff will provide you with a list of researchers who, for a fee, will do the research you require.

★ **Organization.** It is important to be organized in your search if you want to find the information you need as quickly and easily as possible. On the other hand, if you have lots of time and

no particular topic to be researching, browsing can often turn up all sorts of interesting information that you can use at a later date or trade with other researchers. This book will help you to get organized by discussing various resources that are available to you. Feel free to use the margins and the extra spaces in the book for your notes. You may want to list those sources that will be most suited to your research, with little boxes in front of each item that can be checked off after the source is examined. For example:

❒ Send for Captain Linn's service and pension records at the National Archives
❒ Find regimental history for the 51st Pennsylvania Volunteer Infantry
❒ Check local library
❒ Try Interlibrary loan
❒ Check Civil War bibliographies for information on the unit

2

Setting Out On Your Journey

Throughout this book, we will mention libraries and archives frequently. If you don't have much experience beyond visiting your local library, there are a number of things to consider:

★ **Calling ahead.** If traveling some distance, it is always advisable to call or write ahead to obtain a schedule of library hours and regulations. It is also important to explain what you will need to look at, since most places have to pull the manuscript collections in advance (especially at large repositories like Duke University, where they have many, many boxes of holdings). Some repositories require an appointment or prior arrangements to accommodate handicapped visitors. Asking for what you need in advance saves you time, saves the librarians time since they can retrieve the material at their leisure, and will let you know if what you are looking for is actually there, so as to avoid costly mistakes if you are traveling.

> ★——Research Tip——★
>
> **Find out in advance what each library will require in the form of identification. Several libraries I have visited require a photo I.D. for admission. Other libraries require you to fill out an information sheet before they will grant access to you.**

If you are just going for a general "look-see" then it is not necessary to identify specific material in advance, unless the material is locked up in a room that may be closed on certain days or at certain times. Many libraries have very limited hours for their Rare Book Collections and Manuscript Divisions, so always call ahead. We live in an age of downsizing; with limited budgets, many libraries have been forced to curtail hours, especially if there is a staff shortage, so please, always check in advance so you're not surprised or disappointed when you arrive in person.

Some libraries have guides to their manuscript collections that they might send you in advance (rare) or let you examine when you are there. This will help you to be more specific in your request to the librarian for which items you need, since in many cases, a manuscript collection may consist of all of someone's papers from their life, with only a small portion being related to the Civil War and an even smaller portion being relevant to your research. This is often the case with general officers who went on to lead active public lives or hold elected offices.

★ **Pencils and Paper.** Always go prepared with your own paper (or notebook) and writing implements. Many archives and repositories that allow visitors to inspect original Civil War documents only allow you to take notes with a pencil, so always carry plenty of them. Some places, such as the National Archives, also supply you with their own paper and ban researchers from using their own notebooks (for security purposes).

★—Research Tip—★

If you are using a portable computer (laptop), hand copier, or tape recorder, always find out in advance the library's regulations for using such machines. Don't forget extra batteries or tapes if using a recorder.

★ **Clean Hands and No Food.** When working with priceless original documents, be sure your hands are clean and dry. Also, do not take any food or beverage into the library with you. This may seem obvious, but friends who are librarians wanted me to remind you. Be extremely careful, especially when opening or reclosing a document or letter. Some libraries provide special gloves for you to wear when working with original documents, in order to better preserve and protect the documents. It is a privilege to work with original documents, not a right.

★ **Storage Lockers.** You will generally not be allowed to take a briefcase, bag, knapsack, or large purse into most of these facilities. You *may* be allowed to bring in some notes. Many facilities will provide *lockers* for your belongings, often for free—*just don't forget to get your things back before leaving.* Cloakrooms or coat and umbrella stands are provided in some facilities. Another choice is to lock your belongings into your car, but in some neighborhoods this may not be a viable option.

★ **Time Management**. Allow plenty of time for research. Sometimes it may take longer for you to obtain research materials. In archives that allow researchers to examine original documents, you must first dig through a card catalog or other type of finding aid (such as the manuscript guides discussed above) to determine what you want to look at. Then, you fill out a call slip and a library staff person goes and locates the material for you. If the repository is heavily used, this process could take over an hour, so be prepared to wait. Also, other people may happen to be using the material in which you are interested, so always have alternative collections in mind to examine if this should occur. Sometimes you will find stuff that you did not expect to locate, and more time is needed for you to examine relevant documents.

★ **Copying of records**. If your time is limited, always find out in advance the library's photocopying procedure and cost. If you discover that the documents you need are important to your research and you will practically transcribe the document as you take notes, then *it is advantageous for you to pay for copying the entire document rather than spend a long time making copious notes.* You will also have the convenience of examining the material more leisurely, and if you have questions later, you can look at the material again if you have your own copy.

Some libraries will make copies for you immediately; some may require you to fill out a request form, pay in advance, and then send you the copies when the staff has time to make them for you. Some libraries have self-service copiers; in that case always make sure you have the correct change. I always carry rolls of dimes and quarters when making research trips.

Lastly, some libraries have limits on the number of pages you may copy, and some libraries do not allow copying at all. The "no copying" rule generally applies to very fragile documents and bound volumes.

> ★——Research Tip——★
>
> To cope with copying limits, request the maximum number yourself, then have your spouse and other family members request copies. If all else fails, ask a friend, but if the place has a maximum per year, your friend may not want to use up his quota for your research.

★ **Computers**. Computers are wonderful tools for organizing your research and storing massive quantities of data in a small space. They also help conserve paper. However, one drawback is that a power failure will render it unusable, and a power surge can wipe out all your data. So a word to the wise is in order: *Always back up your data with either hard copy (print it out and file it) or a copy on a hard or floppy disk.*

★ **Never Hesitate To Ask Questions**. Library staff members are there to help patrons; if you are confused about locations of books or manuscripts, how to use microfilm machines, or anything else, ask. You will save valuable time by asking questions. There is no such thing as a dumb question!

Some libraries have specialists, including a reference librarian, a book librarian, a manuscripts/special collections librarian, and a photographic collections librarian, each with specialized expertise that can save you an immense amount of time and give you insights you may otherwise miss.

3

Finding the Information You Need

Information can be found in many ways and in many places. The following resources will be discussed in this chapter:

★ People
★ Books
  Primary Sources
  Bibliographies
  Biographies
  Chronologies

Basic Reference Sources

★ Card Catalogs

★ Libraries

★ National Archives

★ Regional Archives

★ State Archives

★ Historical Societies

★ Grand Army of the Republic (GAR) Records

★ Museums

★ Private Collections

★ Town Records

★ Church Records

★ Genealogical Records

★ Census Records

★ Civil War Battlefield Sites

★ Trade Shows

★ Computer Networks

★ Newspapers

Civil War Newspapers

Illustrated Newspapers

Postwar Newspapers

★ Postwar Veterans' Publications

★ Current Magazines, Journals, Newspapers, and Newsletters.

People

In addition to networking, there are several ways to find people who may be able to help you with your research. These include:

★ If you're working on a certain military unit, advertise in local newspapers published in counties or cities where the unit was recruited. You could place a classified ad or write a letter to the editor that can be published in the paper so readers can respond to your request for information.

★ Advertise in *Civil War News.* This leading newspaper publishes a classified-ad section which includes numerous requests for research aid. For a sample copy and ad rates, write to the paper at 234 Monarch Hill Road, Tunbridge, VT 05077; call 802-889-3500; or visit their website: http://civilwarnews.com.

★ Advertise in *Civil War Courier.* For a sample copy and

advertising rates, call 800-418-1861 or 716-873-2594; or write to: 2507 Delaware Avenue, Buffalo, NY 14216; or visit their website at www.civilwarcourier.com.

★ Advertise in the Information Sought column in the bimonthly *Blue & Gray Magazine*. The address is 522 Norton Road, Columbus, OH 43228. Telephone 614-870-1861; Website: www.bluegraymagazine.com.

★ Write a letter to the editor of *Civil War Times Illustrated*, the largest Civil War magazine in circulation. CWTI prints lists of information requests. The address is 6405 Flank Drive, Harrisburg, PA 17112. Their website is: www.civilwartimes.com.

★ If you know of information you need in a distant state or city and can't get there, or want someone to search for you, contact a local *Civil War Round Table* to enlist aid. There are now over 200 CWRTs in the United States, and the number continues to grow. These organizations usually meet monthly and have a speaker on a Civil War-related topic. They sometimes go on tours or host seminars or shows. Write a letter to the organization's address, explain your research, and ask for help. Some members will gladly help you in return for reimbursement of expenses; others may charge you for their time. Either way, such help is priceless. To obtain the names of Round Tables near you, check the Civil War Archive website at www.civilwararchive.com/RNDTABLE/webtable.htm.

★ Contact local reenactors to see if the unit you are working on has been recreated by reenactors. If so, you can contact the reenactment unit and identify yourself, explain your research, and ask if anyone in the group has information he/she is willing to share.

Both the *Civil War News* and *Civil War Courier* print a column listing Civil War events, including reenactments, and several reenactment units advertise for members via these newspapers.

Books

Listed below are those volumes out of some 100,000 Civil War books previously published (with several hundred more appearing each year) which are indispensable to Civil War researchers. Some may be available in your local library, or your librarian can order copies via interlibrary loan. Other possible locations for these references would be a state, county, university, or college library, or historical society.

Primary Sources

Moore, Frank (editor). *Rebellion Record.* 11 volumes plus supplement. NY: G. P. Putnam, D. Van Nostrand, 1861-1873.

A contemporary collection of newspaper reports, casualty lists, poetry, and other accounts of the war, printed while the conflict was in progress.

United States. Naval War Records Office. *Official Records of the Union and Confederate Navies in the War of the Rebellion.* 31 volumes. Washington, DC: Government Printing Office, 1894-1927.

O.R.N. is the basic reference set for researching the operations of Union and Confederate vessels during the war.

📖 United States. Surgeon General's Office. *Medical and Surgical History of the War of the Rebellion.* 3 volumes in 6 parts. Washington, DC, 1875-1883.

These six oversized books contain much information on wounds, treatment, disease, and more. The set has been reprinted by Broadfoot Publishing Company, Wilmington, NC.

📖 United States. War Department. *The War of the Rebellion: A Compilation of the Official Records of the Union and Confederate Armies.* 70 volumes in 128 parts. Washington, DC: Government Printing Office, 1880-1901.

Known simply as the Official Records, or O.R., this is the most important primary document set for Civil War research (and its new supplement, see below). Series I contains battle reports and related correspondence; Series II concerns prisoners of war; Series III contains reports and correspondence of Union authorities; and Series IV the correspondence of Confederate authorities. The War Department also published a companion Atlas to Accompany the Official Records of the Union and Confederate Armies *(Washington, 1891-1895).*
Broadfoot has published a CD-ROM version that contains more than 10,000 corrections and additions to the original set. Guild Press of Indiana (telephone 800-913-9563) has produced "The Civil War CD-ROM, The War of the Rebellion," which is programmed to locate every name, word, or phrase in the O.R.s. The Official Records and the Atlas remain in print and are readily available in many libraries. For an excellent guide to

the atlas, army records, and navy records, see Alan C. and Barbara A. Aimone, A User's Guide to the Official Records of the American Civil War *(Shippensburg, PA: White Mane Publishing Company, 1993).*

📖 *Supplement to the Official Records of the Union and Confederate Armies.* 95 volumes. Wilmington, NC: Broadfoot Publishing Company, 1995-1999.

In 1995, Broadfoot began publishing a supplement to the Official Records. Material includes previously unpublished official reports, correspondence, important courts martial, and unit itineraries. Together, the Official Records sets are the most indispensable sources for authentic Civil War research.

Bibliographies

📖 Allard, Dean C., et al (compilers & editors), *United States Naval History Sources in the United States.* Washington, DC: Naval History Division, Department of the Navy, 1979.

Although somewhat dated and lacking telephone numbers, this state-by-state listing of repositories is not only useful to locate naval history sources, but also for Civil War sources at particular state and local institutions.

📖 *America: History and Life.* Santa Barbara, CA: ABC Clio. Telephone: 800-422-2546.

This useful guide includes an annotated listing of periodical literature gleaned from more than 200 journals. AHL also includes listings of book reviews as well as films, videos, dissertations, and microfilm works. Published five times per year. It is also available on CD rom. Available at most major public and university libraries or visit their website at www.abc-clio.com.

📖 Arnold, Louise (compiler). *The Era of the Civil War: 1820-1876.* Carlisle Barracks, PA: U.S. Army Military History Institute, 1982.

Although dated, this guide includes the printed Civil War material available at the United States Army Military History Institute.

📖 Barbuto, Domenica M., and Kreisel, Martha. *Guide to Civil War Books: An Annotated Selection of Modern Works on the War Between the States.* Chicago, IL: American Library Association, 1996.

Succinct reviews of more than 320 books published from 1974-1994, organized into 32 categories.

📖 Broadfoot, Thomas. *Civil War Books: A Priced Checklist, With Advice.* 5th edition. Wilmington, NC: Broadfoot Publishing Company, 2000.

This new edition replaces the 1996 4th edition. It's an indispensable guide for those of you who collect Civil War titles.

📖 Cole, Garold L. *Civil War Eyewitnesses: An Annotated Bibliography of Books and Articles, 1955-1986.* Columbia, SC: University of South Carolina Press, 1988.

Includes 1,395 published items originally penned by Civil War eyewitnesses. Includes beginning and ending dates for each account, a brief description of contents, and an excellent index.

📖 Coletta, Paolo E. *Annotated Bibliography of U. S. Marine Corps History.* Lanham, MD: University Press of America, 1986.

📖 Coletta, Paolo E. *A Bibliography of American Naval History.* Annapolis, MD: Naval Institute Press, 1981.

📖 Coletta, Paolo E. *A Selected and Annotated Bibliography of American Naval History.* Lanham, MD: University Press of America, 1988.

📖 Coulter, E. Merton. *Travels in the Confederate States, A Bibliography.* Norman, OK, 1948, 1963; reprint edition, Wendell, NC: Broadfoot Publishing Company, 1981.

Coulter presented a synopsis and evaluation of each of 492 books containing insightful descriptions of the Southern Confederacy, written by both Union and Confederate soldiers and civilians.

📖 Dornbusch, Charles E. *Military Bibliography of the Civil War.* 3 volumes. NY: New York Public Library, 1967-1971; 4th volume, Dayton, OH: Press of Morningside, 1987; reprint edition, Saugerties, NY: Hope Farm Press, 1995.

The first three volumes were published together, with a fourth updating the set published in 1987. Together, this invaluable set lists most then-known books, pamphlets, articles, and ephemera concerning military units and operations in the Civil War. Does not include naval topics.

📖 Eicher, David J. *The Civil War in Books: An Analytical Bibliography.* Urbana: University of Illinois Press, 1997.

This new bibliography includes 1,100 books, divided into five categories—battles and campaigns, Union biographies, Confederate biographies, unit histories, and general works. Eicher chose books "universally accepted" as classics, those written by important participants, and modern scholarly works. This book is unsurpassed in terms of critical analysis of the books included in this compilation.

📖 Freeman, Douglas Southall. *The South to Posterity.* New York, NY, 1939, 1951; reprint edition, Wendell, NC: Broadfoot Publishing Company, 1983.

A standard work on Confederate bibliography by an eminent authority.

📖 Freeman, Frank R. *Microbes and Minie Balls: An Annotated Bibliography of Civil War Medicine.* New Brunswick, NJ: Fairleigh-Dickinson University Press, 1995.

A new work that is the standard reference for medical literature of the Civil War.

📖 Harwell, Richard. *The Confederate Hundred: A Bibliophilic Selection of Confederate Books.* Urbana, IL: Beta Phi Mu, 1964; reprint edition, Wendell, NC: Broadfoot Publishing Company, 1982.

An annotated bibliography of the 100 most important Confederate studies.

📖 Harwell, Richard. *In Tall Cotton: The 200 Most Important Confederate Books for the Reader, Researcher and Collector.* Austin, TX: Jenkins Publishing Company, 1978.

📖 Jarboe, Betty M. *Obituaries: A Guide to Sources.* 2nd edition. Boston, MA: G. K. Hall & Company, 1989.

A bibliography, organized by state, of books, articles, and a few manuscripts relating to obituary records.

📖 Lathrop, Norman M. and Mary Lou. *Lathrop Report on Newspaper Indexes.* Wooster, OH: Lathrop Enterprises, 1979-1980 edition.

A relatively scarce publication that includes a number of useful newspaper indexes that cover the Civil War period.

📖 Library of Congress. *National Union List of Manuscripts.*

Annual volumes began in 1959. Participating institutions list their manuscript collections, shelf size of each, and a brief description of their contents. Invaluable guide to search through to see what other libraries may have of interest to your research.

📖 Lynch, Barbara A., and Vajda, John E. *United States Naval History: A Bibliography.* 7th edition. Washington, DC: Naval Historical Center, 1993.

📖 Meredith, Lee W. *Civil War Times and Civil War Times Illustrated 30 Year Comprehensive Index.* Twentynine Palms, CA: Historical Indexes, 1989.

📖 Meredith, Lee W. *Guide to Civil War Periodicals: Volume 1, 1991.* Twentynine Palms, CA: Historical Indexes, 1991; *Volume 2,* 1996.

Complete index of articles, book reviews, editorials, and photographs contained in seven major Civil War publications, 1983-1990; the second volume continues the indexing through 1995.

📖 Moebs, Thomas T. *Confederate States Navy Research Guide: Confederate Naval Imprints Described and Annotated.* Williamsburg, VA: Moebs Publishing Company, 1991.

📖 Mullins, Michael, and Reed, Rowena. *The Union Bookshelf: A Selected Civil War Bibliography.* Wilmington, NC: Broadfoot Publishing Company, 1982.

A guide to Northern material, with 114 annotated titles organized by state, unit histories, and personal reminiscences.

📖 Murdock, Eugene C. *The Civil War in the North: A Selective Annotated Bibliography.* New York: Garland Publishing, Inc., 1987.

Listing includes books and articles on Union military, political, and social history, as well as biographies and personal reminiscences, with invaluable citations to other sources.

📖 Nevins, Allan, et al (editors). *Civil War Books: A Critical Bibliography.* 2 volumes. Baton Rouge, LA: Louisiana State University Press, 1969; reprint edition, Wilmington, NC: Broadfoot Publishing Company, 1996.

A classic reference set with nearly 6,000 books arranged in 15 categories, each tersely annotated by a scholar in the field.

📖 Parrish, Michael, and Willingham, Robert M., Jr. *Confederate Imprints: A Bibliography of Southern Publications from Secession to Surrender*. Austin, TX: Jenkins Publishing Company, 1987.

The standard reference work for material published in the South from 1861-1865.

📖 Sauers, Richard A. *The Gettysburg Campaign, June 3-August 1, 1863: A Comprehensive, Selectively Annotated Bibliography*. Westport, CT: Greenwood Press, 1982.

The only separate bibliography about the campaign and battle, with 2,757 fully-indexed entries. Indispensable for doing research on Gettysburg.

📖 Seagrave, Ronald R. *Civil War Books—Confederate and Union: A Bibliography and Price Guide*. Fredericksburg, VA: Sergeant Kirkland's Museum and Historical Society, 1995.

Reviews of more than 150 modern titles, together with annotated listings of Civil War book dealers, presses, and associations. The most complete bibliography conveniently available. The index is a handy way to find state-by-state histories, rosters, etc.

📖 Smith, Myron J. Jr. *American Civil War Navies: A Bibliography*. Metuchen, NJ: Scarecrow Press, 1972.

📖 United States Civil War Centennial Commission. *A Centennial Bibliography (The Civil War Centennial: A Report to the Congress).* Washington, DC, 1968, pages 63-69.

Useful for a listing of Centennial works produced by federal, state, and local agencies. Prepared under the supervision of Allan Nevins.

📖 United States War Department. *Bibliography of State Participation in the Civil War.* Washington, DC, 1913.

An early effort at gathering together the vast literature of the Civil War. This set is divided by state and contains numerous entries not listed elsewhere.

📖 University Microfilms International. *Comprehensive Dissertation Index, 1861-1972.* Ann Arbor, MI. Telephone: 313-761-4700.

Volume 28 of this set contains history-related dissertations and includes a number of Civil War topics. Keep in mind that dissertations are only listed for those institutions which participate in UMI's program.

📖 University Microfilms International. *Dissertation Abstracts International. Part A: Humanities and Social Sciences.*

This set issues monthly listings of dissertations and abstracts, all of which can be ordered from UMI in paper copy or on microfilm.

📖 Woodworth, Steven E. (editor). *The American Civil War: A Handbook of Literature and Research*. Westport, CT: Greenwood Press, 1996.

Woodworth assembled a team of 49 Civil War scholars to produce this superb bibliography, which consists of nine parts, each subdivided into several component parts. Together, these bibliographical essays cover the important publications relevant to the entire Civil War. An exhaustive appendix includes a listing of publishers and dealers of Civil War material.

📖 Wright, John H. *Compendium of the Confederacy: An Annotated Bibliography*. 2 volumes. Wilmington, NC: Broadfoot Publishing Company, 1989.

An alphabetical listing of books, pamphlets, and periodical articles, with many entries not included in other bibliographies, gathered from dealers catalogs.

📖 *Writings on American History*. Annual volumes begun in 1902 and continue to the present. Currently published by Kraus International Publications, Millwood, NY.

Listing of periodical articles by subject.

Biographies

📖 Allardice, Bruce. *More Generals in Gray*. Baton Rouge, LA: Louisiana State University Press, 1995.

Biographies of 137 generals not appearing in Ezra Warner's Generals in Gray.

📖 Bowman, John S. *Who Was Who in the Civil War*. NY: Random House Value Publishing, 1994.

500 alphabetically arranged biographies of military and civilian leaders. Illustrated.

📖 Callahan, Edward W. (editor). *List of Officers of the Navy of the United States and of the Marine Corps from 1775-1900*. NY: L. R. Hamersly & Company, 1901; reprint edition, Gaithersburg, MD: Olde Soldier Books, 1989.

The most complete source for locating service record information about these officers.

📖 Cogar, William B. *Dictionary of Admirals of the U. S. Navy*. Annapolis, MD: Naval Institute Press, 1989.

Surveys 211 men commissioned admiral from 1862 to 1900. Includes a photograph of each man.

📖 Davis, William C. (editor). *The Confederate General.* 6 volumes. NY: National Historical Society, 1991-1992.

Expanded biographies, photographs, and bibliographies of Southern general officers.

📖 Heitman, Francis B. *Biographical Register and Dictionary of the United States Army, 1789-1903.* 2 volumes. Washington, DC: Government Printing Office, 1903; reprint, Urbana, IL: University of Illinois Press, 1965; reprint, Gaithersburg, MD: Olde Soldier Books, 1988.

This set is useful for locating information on Union Regular Army officers and volunteer generals. It also contains a wealth of additional information, such as a list of captains of light artillery batteries, lists of battle losses from the Revolution to 1901, and some organizational tables.

📖 Hubbell, John T., and Geary, James W. *Biographical Dictionary of the Union: Northern Leaders of the Civil War.* Westport, CT: Greenwood Publishing Group, 1995.

Information on 872 Union men and women, including political leaders, editors, photographers, abolitionists, and others who shaped the war effort.

📖 Hunt, Roger D., and Brown, Jack R. *Brevet Brigadier Generals in Blue.* Gaithersburg, MD: Olde Soldier Books, 1990.

Biographies and photographs of the 1,400 officers who were brevetted brigadier general.

📖 Krick, Robert L. *Lee's Colonels: A Biographical Register of the Field Officers of the Army of Northern Virgin*ia. Dayton, OH: Press of Morningside, revised edition, 1991.

Entries on 1,976 commissioned officers who served with Robert E. Lee. An appendix lists 3,524 officers who served in other CSA units. Does not include those men who were commissioned general officers.

📖 Sifakis, Stewart. *Who Was Who in the Civil War.* NY: Facts on File Publications, 1987.

📖 Sifakis, Stewart. *Who Was Who in the Confederacy.* NY: Facts on File Publications, 1989.

More than 1,000 biographies of major military and political leaders, including 425 generals; includes spies and scouts.

📖 Sifakis, Stewart. *Who Was Who in the Union.* NY: Facts on File Publications, 1988.

Biographies of more than 1,500 leaders, including 583 generals.

📖 Wakelyn, Jon L. *Biographical Dictionary of the Confederate States of America*. Westport, CT: Greenwood Press, 1977.

Includes 651 biographical sketches.

📖 Warner, Ezra J. *Generals in Blue*. Baton Rouge, LA: Louisiana State University Press, 1964.

Biographical sketches of the 583 men who attained the rank of general.

📖 Warner, Ezra J. *Generals in Gray*. Baton Rouge, LA: Louisiana State University Press, 1959.

Biographical sketches of 425 Southern generals.

📖 Warner, Ezra J., and Yearns, Buck. *Biographical Register of the Confederate Congress*. Baton Rouge, LA: Louisiana State University Press, 1975.

Sketches of 267 legislators.

Chronologies

📖 Bowman, John S. *Civil War Almanac*. NY: Facts on File, 1982.

📖 Denny, Robert E. *Civil War Prisons and Escapes: A Day by Day Chronicle.* NY: Sterling Publishing Company, 1993.

📖 Denny, Robert E. *The Civil War Years: A Day by Day Chronicle of the Life of the Nation.* NY: Sterling Publishing Company, 1992.

📖 Long, E. B. *The Civil War Day by Day.* Garden City, NY: Doubleday & Company, 1971.

A chronological summary of the war years, day by day, listing political events as well as battles and skirmishes. Includes an extensive bibliography.

📖 Mosocco, Ronald A. *Chronological Tracking of the American Civil War Per the Official Records of the War of the Rebellion.* 2nd edition. Williamsburg, VA: James River Publications, 1995.

Listing of more than 10,000 events from the O.R.s, accompanied by a selection of maps from the O.R. Atlas.

📖 United States Navy Department. Naval History Division. *Civil War Naval Chronology, 1861-1865.* Washington, DC: U.S. Navy Department, 1961.

*Although this book contains some inaccuracies and undocu-
mented entries, it is still a valuable addition to Civil War naval literature.*

Basic Reference Sources

📖 Ammen, William. *Personnel of the Civil War.* 2 volumes. NY:
Thomas Yoseloff, 1961.

*A retitled reprint of an earlier work that includes an invalu-
able list of local nicknames for Union and Confederate companies and regiments.*

📖 Boatner, Mark M. III. *The Civil War Dictionary.* NY: David
McKay Company, Inc., 1988 (revised edition); softbound
edition, NY: Random House, 1991.

*4,186 alphabetical entries; 2,000 are biographical sketches of
Civil War leaders; 86 maps and diagrams. Covers battles as
well as technical aspects.*

📖 Broadfoot Publishing Company. *The Roster of Confederate
Soldiers 1861-1865.* 16 volumes. Wilmington, NC, 1995-
1996.

*An alphabetical listing of more than 1.5 million names of South-
ern soldiers, including company and regiment of each.*

📖 Broadfoot Publishing Company. *The Roster of Union Soldiers 1861-1865.* 33 volumes. Wilmington, NC, 1996 to date.

This alphabetical listing of more than 3 million names began publication in late 1996. Company and regiment of each soldier are included.

📖 Brown, Brian A. *In the Footsteps of the Blue and Gray: A Civil War Research Handbook.* Shawnee Mission, KS: Two Trails Genealogy Shop, 1996.

A handy guide on identifying ancestors, locating post-war records, military units, and state research sources for both Union and Confederate soldiers and units. A timesaver for beginning researchers.

📖 Coggins, Jack. *Arms and Equipment of the Civil War.* NY: Doubleday & Company, 1962.

A dated but still useful guide designed for the average reader interested in the war.

📖 Current, Richard N. (editor). *Encyclopedia of the Confederacy.* 4 volumes. NY: Simon & Schuster, 1993.

Over 1,400 entries by 300 leading scholars and 4 editors, with over 600 illustrations. Includes bibliographical citations for each entry and provides a cultural, social, and political overview of the Confederacy.

📖 Dyer, Frederick H. *A Compendium of the War of the Rebellion.* Des Moines, IA, 1908; reprinted in 3 volumes, NY: Thomas Yoseloff, 1959; reprinted in 2 volumes, Dayton, OH: Press of Morningside, 1994.

One of the best reference works for researching Union military units. Dyer included capsule histories of most Union regiments, batteries, and other units, as well as a list of battles, organization of Union armies, departments, and districts, and other statistical information such as numbers and losses. Also includes a battle index by state.

📖 Estes, Claud. *List of Field Officers, Regiments and Battalions in the Confederate States Army, 1861-1865.* Macon, GA, 1912.

📖 Evans, Clement A. (editor). *Confederate Military History.* 12 volumes. Atlanta, GA: Confederate Publishing Company, 1899; reprinted several times since by several companies.

A standard reference work that consists of individual state volumes, each written by an expert from that state, and edited by Evans, a former Confederate general. Good material on the home front in each state, as well as on troops from each state and military actions in the South.

📖 Faust, Patricia L. (editor). *Historical Times Illustrated Encyclopedia of the Civil War*. NY: Harper & Row, 1986.

2,380 entries by 62 historians and 5 editors. Has 1,000 illustrations and 67 maps.

📖 Fox, William F. *Regimental Losses in the American Civil War, 1861-1865*. Albany, NY: Albany Publishing Company, 1898; reprint edition, Dayton, OH: Press of Morningside, 1985.

📖 Freeman, Douglas S. *A Calendar of Confederate Papers*. Richmond, VA: The Confederate Museum, 1908; New York, 1969.

Although dated, this classic chronological bibliography of Confederate publications is also a beginning research guide to the papers in the Confederate White House.

📖 Gibson, Charles D. and E. Kay. *Dictionary of Transports and Combatant Vessels, Steam and Sail, Employed by the Union Army, 1861-1868*. Camden, ME: Ensign Press, 1995.

A useful supplement to Civil War naval history, this work lists ships employed by the Union land forces both as combat and transport vessels.

📖 Groene, Bertram H. *Tracing Your Civil War Ancestor*. Winston-Salem, NC: John F. Blair, 1995.

An excellent guide on how to find information on your Civil War military ancestor, both Northern and Southern.

📖 Johnson, Robert U., and Buel, Clarence C. *Battles and Leaders of the Civil War.* 4 volumes. NY: The Century Company, 1884-1888; reprinted several times since.

A basic source book for the entire war, consisting of articles by leading generals as well as other active officers and civilians.

📖 Katcher, Philip. *The Civil War Source Book.* NY: Facts on File Publications, 1992.

Illustrated reference on the armies, battles, and weapons; includes a glossary and a useful essay on published sources. Contains chronology and includes information on graphic arts, photographs, and videos.

📖 Lord, Francis A. *They Fought for the Union.* NY: Bonanza Books, 1960.

A reference work on Union soldiers and sailors.

📖 National Historical Society. *The Image of War: 1861-1865.* 6 volumes. NY, 1982-1984.

A photographic history using thousands of unpublished images, covering the entire war. This set replaces Francis T. Miller's The Photographic History of the Civil War *(1911).*

📖 Neagles, James C. *Confederate Research Sources: A Guide to Archival Collections.* Salt Lake City, UT: Ancestry Inc., 1986.

📖 Neagles, James C. *U. S. Military Records: A Guide to Federal and State Sources, Colonial America to the Present.* Salt Lake City, UT: Ancestry Inc., 1994.

📖 Ripley, Warren. *Artillery and Ammunition of the Civil War.* NY: Bonanza Books, 1970.

📖 *The Roll of Honor.* 27 volumes. Reprint edition, Baltimore: Genealogical Publishing Company, 1994-1996.

Originally published by the Quartermaster's Department between 1865 and 1871, these books provide lists of burials of Union soldiers, organized by cemetery and state. The reprint edition includes a name index compiled by William and Martha Reamy, and a supplemental volume compiled by Mark Hughes, The Unpublished Roll of Honor, *which includes sites missed in the original work (Ball's Bluff, Grafton, and cemeteries in forts and other military posts.)*

Roller, David C., and Twyman, Robert W. (editors). *Encyclopedia of Southern History*. Baton Rouge, LA: Louisiana State University Press, 1979.

Sauers, Richard A. *Advance the Colors! Pennsylvania Civil War Battleflags*. 2 volumes. Harrisburg, PA: Capitol Preservation Committee, 1987-1991.

Excellent reference on Pennsylvania regiments and Civil War flags.

Segars, J. H. *In Search of Confederate Ancestors: The Guide*. Murfreesboro, TN: Southern Heritage Press, 1993.

A basic, though comprehensive, approach to doing genealogical work on Confederate soldiers.

Sibley, F. Ray Jr. *The Confederate Order of Battle: The Army of Northern Virginia*. Shippensburg, PA: White Mane Press, 1995.

An examination of the organization of Lee's army, battle by battle. A forthcoming volume will detail other Confederate armies.

Sifakis, Stewart. *Compendium of the Confederate Armies*. 10 volumes. NY: Facts on File Publications, 1992-1994.

A new series that presents information on each Confederate unit, including commanders, area of recruitment, dates of service, battles, and more. Generally, a Confederate equivalent to Dyer's Compendium. Volumes organized by state.

📖 Silverstone, Paul H. *Warships of the Civil War Navies.* Annapolis, MD: Naval Institute Press, 1989.

A standard reference work, heavily illustrated, for both navies, following the format used by the modern Jane's series.

📖 Todd, Frederick P. *American Military Equipage, 1851-1872.* 2 volumes. Providence, RI, 1974; reprint edition, Dayton, OH: Morningside Press, 1995.

A state-by-state, as well as Regular Army, examination of equipment, uniforms, and insignia used during the period covered.

📖 *The Union Army.* 8 volumes. Madison, WI: Federal Publishing Company, 1908; reprint edition in 9 volumes (new index), Wilmington, NC: Broadfoot Publishing Company, 1998.

This set contains capsule unit histories for all units from Northern states, as well as biographical sketches, lists of battles, and a naval volume.

📖 United States Adjutant General's Office. *Official Army Register of the Volunteer Force of the U.S. Army for the Years 1861-*

1865. 8 volumes. Washington, DC, 1865-67; reprint edition, Gaithersburg, MD: Ron R. Van Sickle Military Books, 1987.

Lists all commissioned officers of Union volunteer units, organized by state. A ninth volume added to the reprint provides a useful index.

📖 Welcher, Frank J. *The Union Army, 1861-1865: Organizations and Operations*. 2 volumes. Bloomington, IN: Indiana University Press, 1987-1992.

Histories and extensive organizational data on Union armies, corps, divisions, and brigades. Volume 1 covers the area east of the Appalachians, Volume 2 the western theater.

📖 Wiley, Bell I., and Milhollen, Hirst D. *They Who Fought Here*. NY: Bonanza Books, 1969.

A good introduction to the common soldier of both sides.

Card Catalogs

These are available at some libraries in the traditional paper-cards-in-wooden-trays or on computer. Most large libraries and university libraries also have their card catalog available on the internet. Browse through them, looking at any sections that may be relevant. Most libraries use the standard *Library of Congress Subject Headings* (Washington: Library of Congress, 21st edition in 5 volumes, 1998). The standard heading to look under first is: United States–History–Civil War; followed by subheadings such as: Battles, Campaigns, Poetry, and Bibliographies.

Also, check the card catalog for other headings, such as the specific name of a battle, person, or place. Don't forget to check under United States Army–History, and United States Navy–History, for holdings in these and related categories. Look under Confederate States, followed by subheadings, for related topics.

> ★—Research Tip—★
>
> Be sure to read the bibliographies at the end of the books. This is a great source for more references for your research.

Try to think up as many possible headings for which the information you seek may be filed. One interesting note is that computer card catalogs tend to be very inaccurate; many times I have found books on the shelves that do not appear in the card catalog. Remember, a computer is only as good as the person entering the data, so you need to think like a variety of people.

Libraries file their books using one of two major systems—Dewey Decimal or Library of Congress. In the Dewey Decimal system, Civil War books can be found in the section containing books labeled 973.7. The Library of Congress system starts with E470 for Civil War books.

Once you have found the numbers for the sections you are interested in, go to that section and look at each book's spine. If the spine is unlabeled, open the book to see what it is. Pull all relevant books (a few at a time, if necessary) and take them to a research table in the library to examine at greater length. You may ask the librarians to loan you a cart to carry your books. Also scan a few shelves before and after the numbers you are looking for to allow for shelving errors.

Also, be sure to ask the librarians if there is more Civil War material anywhere else in the library, such as a Rare Book room, Genealogy room, Special Collections room, vertical files (collections of pamphlets, newspaper clippings, magazine articles, and other such material usually organized by topic), newspapers, or photographs.

Libraries

The Civil War has generated thousands of books since 1865, along with countless magazine and journal articles, photographs, artifacts, and other ephemera. Almost every library in the country has some type of Civil War collection among its books, and there are specialized libraries that have nothing but Civil War material to assist the determined researcher.

The standard guide to American libraries is the *American Library Directory* (now in its 50th edition, 1997-1998, 2 volumes, New Providence, NJ: R. R. Bowker). Libraries are listed by state, then by city or town.

For a convenient reference guide to libraries having manuscripts, take a look at National Historical Publications and Records Commission, *Directory of Archives and Manuscript Repositories in the United States* (Phoenix, NY: Oryx Press, 1988). Still useful, though dated, is Philip M. Hamer's *A Guide to Archives and Manuscripts in the United States* (New Haven, CT: Yale University Press, 1961).

Lee Ash's *Subject Collections* (7th edition, 2 volumes, New Providence, NJ: R. R. Bowker, 1993) is also useful. Ash lists libraries having special collections in a wide variety of topics, including Civil War history. Most larger libraries will have copies of these volumes.

★—Research Tip—★

Be sure to read footnotes and bibliographies to obtain leads on manuscript collections, books, and articles which may be of help to your research.

Some Specialized Civil War Libraries and Repositories with Exceptional Civil War Holdings

🏛 Charles L. Blockson African-American Collection, Temple University, Sullivan Hall 007-01, Philadelphia, PA 19122. Telephone: 215-204-6632.
Website:www.library.temple.edu/blockson

This vastly important collection contains more than 25,000 volumes, 3,500 rare books, and over 15,000 other pieces pertaining to Afro-American history. The John Brown Collection includes material on the Abolition Society of Pennsylvania, while the Underground Railroad Collection has more than 1,000 items. More than 100 items reside in the Slave Narrative Collection.

🏛 Civil War Library & Museum, 1805 Pine Street, Philadelphia, PA 19103. Telephone: 215-735-8196.
E-mail:cwlm@netreach.net
Website: www.netreach.net/~cwlm

Located south of Rittenhouse Square, this library was originally established by the Military Order of the Loyal Legion of the United States (MOLLUS), a postwar Union officers' organization. The CWLM has an excellent book and pamphlet collection, a number of artifacts (such as General George G. Meade's sword, uniform, and headquarters flags), photographs, and manuscripts.

🏛 Duke University, William R. Perkins Library, Durham, NC 27708. Telephone: 919-660-5822.
Website: http://scriptorium.lib.duke.edu

Duke has an outstanding collection of Civil War-related manuscript collections. The published guide is by Richard C. Davis & Linda A. Miller, Guide to the Cataloged Collections in the Manuscript Department of the William R. Perkins Library, Duke University *(Santa Barbara, CA: Clio Books, 1980).*

🏛 George Tyler Moore Center for the Study of the Civil War, Shepherd College, Shepherdstown, WV 25443. Telephone: 304-876-5429. Website: www.shepherd.edu\gtmcweb\

★—Research Tip—★

Be sure to check the more general periodical indexes, such as *Reader's Guide to Periodical Literature*, *Social Sciences Index*, and *Humanities Index*, among others that your local library may have.

The mission of the center is to promote scholarly research on the Civil War through the development of a database that holds vital statistics about Union and Confederate soldiers, sailors, and marines. The center also is developing educational programs and publications on the Civil War.

🏛 Hill College, P.O. Box 619, Hillsboro, TX 76645. Telephone: 254-582-2555, extension 246.

This small college is host to the Texas Heritage Museum, which has acquired a number of valuable Civil War manuscript collections and maintains a specialized library.

🏛 Historical Society of Pennsylvania, 1300 Locust Street, Philadelphia, PA 19107. Telephone: 215-732-6200. Website: www.libertynet.org/pahist/

Among the society's numerous manuscript holdings are the papers of George G. Meade, Andrew A. Humphreys, George A. McCall, William B. Rawle, Sullivan A. Meredith, and William F. Biddle (one of General McClellan's aides). In 1991, the society published the Guide to the Manuscript Collections of the Historical Society of Pennsylvania.

🏛 Henry E. Huntington Library, 1151 Oxford Road, San Marino, CA 91108. Telephone: 626-405-2141 or 626-405-2125. Website: www.huntington.org

This library contains the papers of General Joseph Hooker and the important John P. Nicholson Collection. Nicholson served in the 28th PA during the Civil War, was prominent in the GAR and MOLLUS, and was one of the three commissioners of the Gettysburg Battlefield when the park was transferred to Federal control in 1893. Nicholson acquired an immense personal collection of books and papers, and the Huntington Library has custody of this material. Nicholson himself published a bibliography of his collection; it is useful to read through this volume because Nicholson inserted autographed letters from veterans into their books. These letters are sometimes important, as are the one-of-a-kind items that Nicholson collected in book form, such as some newspaper clippings books. Nicholson published a guide to his book collection, Catalogue of the Library of Brevet Lieutenant-Colonel John Page Nicholson *(Philadelphia, 1914; reprint edition, Storrs-Mansfield, CT: Maurizio Martino Publisher, 1995).*

🏛 Library of Congress, Manuscripts Division, James Madison Memorial Building, First Street and Independence Avenue SE, Washington, DC 20540. Telephone: 202-707-5387. Website: lcweb.loc.gov/rr/mss

Among the library's outstanding Civil War papers are those of Abraham Lincoln, George B. McClellan, U. S. Grant, Jubal A. Early, John A. Dahlgren, David D. Porter, Fitz-John Porter, Henry A. Hunt, and hundreds of other participants. The library has a number of original Civil war maps as well as the Brady Collection of photographs. See Dr. John R. Sellers, Civil War Manuscripts: A Guide to the Collections in the Manuscript Division of the Library of Congress *(Washington, 1986) for details on the library's holdings.*

🏛 Naval Historical Center, Washington Navy Yard, 805 Kidder Breeze SE, Washington, DC 20374-5060. Telephone: 202-433-2765. Website: www.history.navy.mil

The Naval Historical Center contains an extensive reference library as well as an outstanding photograph collection. The Naval Historical Foundation provides photograph copying services to the public provided that each request must first go through the Naval Historical Center to ascertain photo availability and identification numbers. Call for more information. The library's published manuscript guide is Naval Historical Foundation Manuscript Collection: A Catalog *(Washington, DC: Library of Congress, 1974).*

🏛 Soldiers & Sailors Memorial Hall, 4141 Fifth Avenue, Pittsburgh, PA 15213. Telephone: 412-621-4253. Website: www.soldiersandsailorshall.org

This building was erected through a collaborative effort of the city's GAR posts, and contains a reference library, photographs, artifacts, and manuscripts.

🏛 United States Army Military History Institute, 22 Ashburn Drive, Carlisle, PA 17013. Telephone: 717-245-3611 (reference), 717-245-3434 (photos), 717-245-3601 (archives). Website: http://carlisle-www.army.mil/usamhi/

Formed in the late 1960s, the USAMHI houses a large Civil War book and pamphlet collection. The Archives, headed by Dr. Richard J. Sommers, has one of the largest Civil War manuscript collections in the country. The Photograph Archives maintains custody of the Massachusetts MOLLUS Collection of more than 300 Civil War photo albums, and is actively copying images loaned by private collectors.

🏛 United States Civil War Center, Louisiana State University, Baton Rouge, LA 70803-5111. Telephone: 225-388-3151. Website: http://www.cwc.lsu.edu

Under the direction of David Madden, the center is building upon LSU's major Civil War collection, as well as T. Michael Parrish's Confederate Imprints database, and is developing a

computerized database of Civil War collections of books, imprints, letters, diaries, manuscripts, maps, photographs, and artwork located throughout the United States. The center also makes available an Internet World Wide Web homepage and links over 800 Civil War institutions and organizations (including existing catalogs of collections and the National Park Service database of vital statistics of Civil War soldiers).

United States Marine Corps Historical Center, Washington Navy Yard SE, Building 558, Washington, DC 20374. Telephone: 202-433-3534. Website: www.hqmc.usmc.mil

The USMC Historical Center is the place to go in search of information about the history of the corps.

United States Military Academy Library, West Point, NY 10996. Telephone: 914-938-2954.

The library at West Point is open for public research and contains an extensive research collection of U.S. military history books. The Archives (914-938-7052) has a good collection of Civil War-related manuscript collections.

United States Naval Institute Library, 118 Maryland Avenue, Annapolis, MD 21402. Telephone: 410-268-6110. Website: www.usni.org

The Naval Institute's library has a large collection of Civil War naval books as well as photos.

University of North Carolina, Manuscript Department, Campus Box 3926, Wilson Library, Chapel Hill, NC 27514. Telephone: 919-962-1345. Website: www.lib.unc.edu/mss

The Wilson Library (Room 024-A) houses the Southern Historical Collection of manuscripts, which includes a sizeable number of Civil War papers. The library also houses the Center for the Study of the American South, one of the nation's most impressive arrays of Southern materials, photographs, and recordings. The SHC's published guide is Susan S. Blosser and Clyde N. Wilson Jr.'s, The Southern Historical Collection: A Guide to Manuscripts *(1970), and Everard H. Smith III's,* The Southern Historical Collection: Supplementary Guide to Manuscripts, 1970-1975 *(1976).*

 Western Reserve Historical Society, 10825 East Boulevard, Cleveland, OH 44106. Telephone: 216-721-5722. Website: www.wrhs.org

Of importance here is the William P. Palmer Collection. Palmer sent out agents to buy Civil War material earlier this century; the result is this collection, which includes material on Union and Confederate regiments from thirty states as well as a large number of miscellaneous manuscripts, bound volumes, and photographs. The society has several unpublished finding aids for the Palmer Collection; call in advance for more details and request copies of selected guides.

For a general guide to the society's holdings, see Kermit J. Pike's A Guide to the Manuscripts and Archives of the Western Reserve Historical Society *(1972).*

The above list is by no means exhaustive. It pays to contact as many libraries and archives as your time permits to see what they have pertaining to your topic. Keep in mind that budgetary constraints have forced some libraries to cut services and the hours they are open for public use; it is always advisable to contact them in advance for hours of operation, and, if possible, write for information on a specific topic.

The National Archives

8th & Pennsylvania Avenue NW, Washington, DC 20408. Telephone: 202-501-5400—Military Reference Branch: 202-501-5390 x278; Old Navy Branch: x227.

Still Picture Branch (photos, images, drawings) is at 8601 Adelphi Road, College Park, MD 20740-6001. Telephone 301-713-6625.

Cartographic Branch (maps) is at 8601 Adelphi Road, College Park, MD 20740-6001. Telephone: 301-713-7030.

Website: www.nara.gov

At some point in your research, you will probably either have to go to Washington for research there, or order copies of records (paper or microfilm) by mail. The National Archives, simply put, has the largest collection of Civil War records in America, and serious Civil War research cannot be done without checking the National Archives for information on your subject.

> ★—Research Tip—★
>
> Records at the National Archives are divided into record groups by federal agencies—referred to as RG.

The federal records maintained by the National Archives are divided into record groups, each group pertaining to one federal agency. Of the more than 400 record groups, *more than 80 of them contain important Civil War material.* The following record groups contain the most important Civil War records:

★ RG 15, Records of the Veterans Administration
   Includes Civil War pension records.

★ RG 19, Records of the Bureau of Ships
   Material on ship construction, equipment, and repairs.

★ RG 24, Records of the Bureau of Naval Personnel

★ RG 45, Naval Records Collection of the Office of Naval
   Records and Library

★ RG 56, General Records of the Department of the
   Treasury

★ RG 77, Records of the Office of the Chief of Engineers

★ RG 92, Records of the Office of the Quartermaster
   General

★ RG 94, Records of the Adjutant General's Office, 1780–
   1917

★ RG 99, Records of the Office of the Paymaster General

★ RG 107, Records of the Office of the Secretary of War

★ RG 109, War Department Collection of Confederate
   Records

★ RG 110, Records of the Provost Marshal General's Bureau

★ RG 111, Records of the Office of the Chief Signal
   Officer
   Includes the 6,000-image Brady Collection of photographs.

★ RG 112, Records of the Office of the Surgeon General

★ RG 123, Records of the United States Court of Claims
Material on claims made against the federal government for damages suffered during the war.

★ RG 127, Records of the United States Marine Corps

★ RG 153, Records of the Office of the Judge Advocate General
Court-martial records are included in this group.

★ RG 181, Records of Naval Districts and Shore Establishment.

★ RG 217, Records of the General Accounting Office

★ RG 249, Records of the Commissary General of Prisoners

★ RG 391, Records of United States Regular Army Mobile Units, 1821-1942

★ RG 393, Records of United States Army Continental Commands, 1821-1920
This includes records of armies, corps, and their constituent units—divisions and brigades. Regimental records are in RG 94.

The Archives has published two major guides to facilitate research. They are:

📖 *Guide to Federal Archives Relating to the Civil War*, by Kenneth W. Munden & Henry P. Beers (Washington: Government Printing Office, 1962), which was reprinted in 1982 as *The Union: A Guide to Federal Archives Relating to the Civil War*;

📖 *Guide to the Archives of the Government of the Confederate States of America*, by Henry P. Beers (Washington: Government Printing Office, 1968), which was reprinted in 1982 as *The Confederacy: A Guide to the Archives of the Confederate States of America.*

Both volumes provide a wealth of details on the contents of each record group, as well as supporting bibliographies to enable the researcher to locate additional information on each agency. Each volume, especially the CSA guide, also includes notes of related records held by other repositories.

📖 The Archives has also published *Military Service Records: A Select Catalog of National Archives Microfilm Publications* (Washington, 1985). This guide lists contents of microfilm reels available for purchase from the National Archives, records from the Revolutionary War through the 1898 War with Spain. If your local library does not have a copy of this guide, it can be ordered from the U. S. Government Printing Office.

📖 Finally, if you are looking for Civil War maps, examine *A Guide to Civil War Maps in the National Archives* (Washington, 1986), for information on the types of maps available to researchers.

In general, anyone researching any Civil War unit should contact the Military Reference Branch of the National Archives to inquire about what records for that unit are available. The Civil War army was awash in paperwork—there were forms for everything—and much of that paperwork is still available for research. In fact, the amount of surviving material relating to one regiment can be both astounding and overwhelming. For example, one regiment might have material contained in several record groups. Muster rolls are in RG 94 (Adjutant General's Office), as are regimental books and papers. RG 393 contains records of brigades, divisions, corps, and armies, so researchers should also check this RG for information on higher echelons in which a particular unit served.

★—Research Tip—★

For copies of National Archives publications, contact the National Archives Bookstore at 800-234-8861 or 202-501-5235. The bookstore will send you a free catalog upon request.

Michael P. Musick, an outstanding Civil War specialist in the Military Reference Branch, has written an excellent series of articles concerning Civil War research at the Archives. All are published in *Prologue: Quarterly of the National Archives:*

📖 "Civil War Records: An Introduction and Invitation." 27 #2 (Summer 1995): 145-50.

📖 "The Little Regiment: Civil War Units and Commands." 27 #2 (Summer 1995): 151-71.

📖 "Honorable Reports: Battles, Campaigns, and Skirmishes—Civil War Records and Research." 27 #3 (Fall 1995): 258-77.

📖 "War in an Age of Numbers: Civil War Arms and Equipment." 27 #4 (Winter 1995): 348-68.

📖 "Local History Sources—Civil War," To appear in a future issue.

★—Research Tip—★

Make sure you read material (reports, regimental histories, biographies, etc.) about troops that opposed the unit you are working on; often, even if the opposition did not mention your unit by name and number, your unit was described or mentioned in reports and related material.

One of the most popular requests that the National Archives receives each year is for *military and pension records of individual soldiers.* Photocopies of such documents can be obtained from the archives by using NATF Form 80 (see example, page 71). Some libraries stock copies of this form for patrons; you can obtain a supply of these forms by writing to:

The National Archives
General Reference Branch (NNRG-P)
8th & Pennsylvania Avenues NW
Washington, DC 20408

By using this form, you can request copies of service and pension records for soldiers who served in volunteer Union regiments during the Civil War. Requests for information about Regular Army officers and men is more difficult because there are no separate service records for the regulars. Information on Confederate soldiers is also available. If researching an ancestor contact the Military Reference Branch (202-501-5390).

NATF-80 forms are used to request both compiled service records and pension records of individual soldiers. After the war, as pension requests inundated the Adjutant General's Office, it became clear that continued use of original documents would result in their destruction. Therefore, the office began a lengthy program in which an army of clerks went through all muster rolls, hospital registers, and other wartime forms. Each soldier's name was copied onto specially-created cards. When completed, the cards for each soldier show his entire service record without need to consult original forms. This was done for most Union soldiers. The National Archives undertook a similar project in the 1920s for Confederate troops as well.

The Archives also has custody of pension records for Union veterans. If searching for any postwar pension information about a Confederate soldier, you should contact the state archives in the state from which the soldier served, as Southern states usually awarded pensions to needy veterans in gray, as well as their widows.

The illustration on page 71 shows NATF Form 80. You must fill out separate forms if you request both the compiled service record and pension information for the same soldier. If the person whose data you are requesting served in more than one unit, you must also fill out a separate NATF Form 80 for each unit (the compiled service records are filed by unit).

The directions for filling out this form includes the following statement: "When we are unable to provide copies of all pension documents because of the size of a pension application file, we will send copies of the documents we think will be most useful to you for genealogical purposes." In other words, when you send in a request for pension information, the archives staff will not copy an entire file if it is quite thick (as many are). Thus, if you want all the documents in the file, you should write "ENTIRE" after you check the Pension box in Block 1 of the form. When the copying person sees this notation, he or she will copy the entire file and the archives will inform you of the additional cost beyond the basic $10 fee per request.

NATF Form 80

ORDER FOR COPIES OF VETERANS RECORDS
(See Instructions page before completing this form)

DATE RECEIVED IN NNRG

INDICATE BELOW THE TYPE OF FILE DESIRED AND THE METHOD OF PAYMENT PREFERRED.

1. FILE TO BE SEARCHED (Check one box only)
- ☐ PENSION
- ☐ BOUNTY-LAND WARRANT APPLICATION (Service before 1856 only)
- ☐ MILITARY

2. PAYMENT METHOD (Check one box only)
☐ CREDIT CARD (VISA or MasterCard) for IMMEDIATE SHIPMENT of copies
Account Number: _____   Exp. Date: ____
Signature: _____   Daytime Phone: ____
☐ BILL ME (No Credit Card)

REQUIRED MINIMUM IDENTIFICATION OF VETERAN - MUST BE COMPLETED OR YOUR ORDER CANNOT BE SERVICED

3. VETERAN (Give last, first, and middle names)

4. BRANCH OF SERVICE IN WHICH HE SERVED
☐ ARMY   ☐ NAVY   ☐ MARINE CORPS

5. STATE FROM WHICH HE SERVED

6. WAR IN WHICH, OR DATES BETWEEN WHICH, HE SERVED

7. IF SERVICE WAS CIVIL WAR,
☐ UNION   ☐ CONFEDERATE

PLEASE PROVIDE THE FOLLOWING ADDITIONAL INFORMATION, IF KNOWN

8. UNIT IN WHICH HE SERVED (Name of regiment or number, company, etc, name of ship)

9. IF SERVICE WAS ARMY, ARM IN WHICH HE SERVED
☐ INFANTRY   ☐ CAVALRY   ☐ ARTILLERY   If other, specify:

Rank ☐ OFFICER   ☐ ENLISTED

10. KIND OF SERVICE ☐ VOLUNTEERS   ☐ REGULARS

11. PENSION/BOUNTY-LAND FILE NO.

12. IF VETERAN LIVED IN A HOME FOR SOLDIERS, GIVE LOCATION (City and State)

13. PLACE(S) VETERAN LIVED AFTER SERVICE

14. DATE OF BIRTH

15. PLACE OF BIRTH (City, County, State, etc.)

18. NAME OF WIDOW OR OTHER CLAIMANT

16. DATE OF DEATH

17. PLACE OF DEATH (City, County, State, etc.)

NATIONAL ARCHIVES TRUST FUND BOARD   NATF Form 80 (rev. 4-92)

DO NOT WRITE BELOW - SPACE IS FOR OUR REPLY TO YOU

☐ **NO--We were unable to locate the file you requested above. No payment is required.**

DATE SEARCHED	SEARCHER

☐ **REQUIRED MINIMUM IDENTIFICATION OF VETERAN WAS NOT PROVIDED.** Please complete blocks 3 (give full name), 4, 5, 6, and 7 and resubmit your order.

☐ **A SEARCH WAS MADE BUT THE FILE YOU REQUESTED ABOVE WAS NOT FOUND.** When we do not find a record for a veteran, this does not mean that he did not serve. You may be able to obtain information about him from the archives of the State from which he served.

☐ See attached forms, leaflets, or information sheets.

☐ **YES--We located the file you requested above. We have made copies from the file for you. The cost for these copies is $10.**

DATE SEARCHED	SEARCHER
FILE DESIGNATION	

Make your check or money order payable to NATIONAL ARCHIVES TRUST FUND. Do not send cash. Return this form and your payment in the enclosed envelope to:

NATIONAL ARCHIVES TRUST FUND
P.O. BOX 100221
ATLANTA, GA 30384-0221

PLEASE NOTE: We will hold these copies awaiting receipt of payment for only 45 days from the date completed, which is stamped below. After that time, you must submit another form to obtain photocopies of the file.

THIS IS YOUR MAILING LABEL. PRESS FIRMLY.
NAME (Last, First, MI)
STREET
CITY, STATE   ZIP CODE

A616175

INVOICE/REPLY COPY - DO NOT DETACH

Regional Archives

In addition to the holdings in Washington, the National Archives maintains several regional archives centers which contain records and microfilm copies of material related to that particular region of the country. These regional centers are as follows:

★ National Archives–New England Region
  380 Trapelo Road
  Waltham, MA 02452-6399
  Telephone: 781-647-8104
  Website: www.nara.gov/regional/boston.html

★ National Archives–Pittsfield Region
  10 Conte Drive
  Pittsfield, MA 01201-8230
  Telephone: 413-445-6885
  Website: www.nara.gov/regional/pittsfie.html

★ National Archives–Northeast Region
  201 Varick Street
  New York, NY 10014-4811
  Telephone: 212-337-1300
  Website: www.nara.gov/regional/newyork.html

★ National Archives–Mid Atlantic Region
  GSA Regional Office Building
  900 Market Street
  Philadelphia, PA 19107-4292

Telephone: 215-597-3000
Website: www.nara.gov/regional/philacc.html

★ National Archives–Southeast Region
1557 St. Joseph Avenue
East Point, GA 30344
Telephone: 404-763-7474
Website: www.nara.gov/regional/atlanta.html

★ National Archives–Great Lakes Region
7358 South Pulaski Road
Chicago, IL 60629-5898
Telephone: 773-581-7816
Website: www.nara.gov/regional/chicago.html

★ National Archives–Central Plains Region
2312 East Bannister Road
Kansas City, MO 64131-3011
Telephone: 816-926-6272
Website: www.nara.gov/regional/kansas.html

★ National Archives–Southwest Region
501 West Felix Street
P.O. Box 6216
Fort Worth, TX 76115-0216
Telephone: 817-334-5525
Website: www.nara.gov/regional/ftworth.html

★ National Archives–Rocky Mountain Region
Building 48
Denver Federal Center

West 6th Avenue and Kipling Street
P.O. Box 25307
Denver, CO 80225-0307
Telephone: 303-236-0817
Website: www.nara.gov/regional/denver.html

★ National Archives–Pacific Southwest Region
24000 Avila Road
P.O. Box 6719
Laguna Niguel, CA 92677-6719
Telephone: 949-360-2626
Website: www.nara.gov/regional/laguna.html

★ National Archives–Pacific Sierra Region
1000 Commodore Drive
San Bruno, CA 94066-2350
Telephone: 650-876-9001
Website: www.nara.gov/regional/sanfranc.html

★ National Archives–Pacific Northwest Region
6125 Sand Point Way NE
Seattle, WA 98115
Telephone: 206-526-6507
Website: www.nara.gov/regional/seattle.html

★ National Archives–Alaska Region
654 West 3rd Avenue
Anchorage, AK 99501-2145
Telephone: 907-271-2441
Website: www.nara.gov/regional/anchorag.html

Before visiting, call ahead and ascertain if a particular branch has a printed guide to its Civil War holdings. Remember, material relevant to your research may turn up in one of these centers. For example, the Mid-Atlantic regional Archives in Philadelphia has Civil War records from surrounding states, including Maryland and Virginia. This archives center also has a handy published guide to its Civil War records.

State Archives

Virtually every state has a State Archives, which generally possesses all kinds of great reference material. Sometimes, there are guides to the holdings of the State Archives (such as in Pennsylvania) that you can purchase in advance and review. The appendix of this book lists all state archives, addresses, and telephone numbers. This listing also includes state libraries. When you get to the state archives, utilize their finding aids such as catalogs and guides to help you find what you need. As always, feel free to ask a librarian for assistance.

Historical Societies

Most states have a state historical society that contains records relating to that state. Most have extensive groupings of both state (public) and private manuscript collections. The Appendix lists state historical societies. Many counties have local historical societies, and several ethnic societies also actively collect manuscripts. Most cities have historical offices, as do several national organizations and businesses. For more historical societies, consult your phone book or directory (there is a Directory of Historical Societies published by the American Historical Association) or network to find them.

Grand Army of the Republic (GAR) Records

Formed in 1866, the Grand Army of the Republic became the largest Union army veterans' organization of its time. By 1890, almost 500,000 men belonged and thousands more supported its causes, which included aiding needy veterans or their widows and children, obtaining government aid for veterans (pensions), fraternal feeling among veterans, and encouragement of public allegiance to the government. Local soldiers organized GAR posts in practically all Northern states and in Southern states where large numbers of veterans settled after the war. Posts used an elaborate system of oaths and rituals, and kept detailed records in a variety of officially sanctioned books. As the GAR waned, post books and records sometimes disappeared or were donated to local historical societies, state agencies, or were acquired by other veterans' groups such as the American Legion or Veterans of Foreign Wars. Don't forget to check with local veterans' organizations to see if there are GAR records still surviving and unreported.

Researchers working on regimental histories will profit by examining surviving GAR post books. Among the most prominent books used by individual posts were the large, oversized books in which each post member had a page to inscribe with his service record. When properly filled out, each such book became

---

★—Research Tip—★
If you're working on a particular unit, don't forget to read material about other units in the same brigade, division, and corps, for such material often contains references to the unit you're working on.

a goldmine of information about Union soldiers and their memories.

📖 See also, for general information on the GAR, Stuart McConnell, *Glorious Contentment: The Grand Army of the Republic, 1865-1900* (Chapel Hill, NC: University of North Carolina Press, 1992).

GAR Posts of Special Interest

Captain Thomas Espy Post 153
Andrew Carnegie Free Library
300 Beechwood Avenue
Carnegie, PA 15106
Telephone: 412-276-3456
Website: www.clpgh.org/ein/andrcarn

The Espy Post contains a library, numerous Civil War artifacts, and records of the members of the post.

Grand Army of the Republic Civil War Museum & Library
4278 Griscom Street
Philadelphia, PA 19124
Telephone: 215-289-6484

This library, located in an 18th century building, houses the remnants of the city's GAR post libraries and papers. It also has a collection of artifacts, photographs, and manuscripts. The museum is open limited hours, so always call for information.

Ezra S. Griffin Post
GAR Building, 2nd Floor,
305 Linden Street
Scranton, PA 18505

This post library includes a complete collection of Griffin Post papers (founded 1879) as well as a large photograph collection of its members.

GAR Memorial Hall
The Chicago Public Library, Special Collections and
    Preservation Division
400 South State Street
Chicago, IL 60605
Telephone: 312-747-4022
Website: www.chipublib.org

GAR collection contains artifacts, 8,000 volumes, manuscripts, photographs, and other material.

Wisconsin Veterans Museum
30 West Mifflin Street, Room 200
Madison, WI 53702
Telephone: 608-266-1680

Contains Wisconsin Civil War and GAR material, including a fine collection of GAR post records (1883-1930).

Fire Museum of Trenton
244 Perry Street
Trenton, NJ 08618
Telephone: 609-989-4038

This museum contains New Jersey GAR records, photographs, and a Sons of Union Veterans collection.

Soldiers and Sailors Memorial Hall
4141 Fifth Avenue
Pittsburgh, PA 15213
Telephone: 412-621-4253
Website: www.soldiersandsailorshall.org

SSMH contains records of more than a dozen GAR posts in Allegheny County. The hall also has records of other veterans organizations, including the Union Veteran Legion, Grand Army Association, Veteran Guard of Allegheny County, Sons of Union Veterans, and more.

Museums

Many museums have libraries that are open to the public. The American Association of Museums publishes a guide to American Museums that is widely available at larger public and academic libraries.

Some museums that deserve special mention are:

Atlanta History Center
130 West Paces Ferry Road
Atlanta, GA 30305
Telephone: 404-814-4000
Website: www.atlhist.org

Civil War Library and Museum
1805 Pine Street
Philadelphia, PA 19103
Telephone: 215-735-8196

Confederate Museum
929 Camp Street
New Orleans, LA 70130
Telephone: 504-523-4522
Website: www.confederatemuseum.com

Confederate Naval Museum
P.O. Box 1022
Columbus, GA 31902
Telephone: 706-327-9798
Website: www.portcolumbus.org

Museum of the Confederacy
1201 East Clay Street
Richmond, VA 23219
Telephone: 804-649-1861
Website: www.moc.org

While Freeman's calendar (see page 46) is still a useful starting point to the museum library's collections, the library now contains over 5,000 volumes and 675 cubic feet of other materials. In-house guides exist for some collections (Jefferson Davis, Robert E. Lee, Stonewall Jackson). Access to library is by appointment only. Contact Gary R. Swanson (Librarian) or Malinda W. Collier (Director of Collections).

National Museum of Civil War Medicine
P.O. Box 470
48 East Patrick Street
Frederick, MD 21705
Telephone: 301-695-1864
Website: www.civilwarmed.org

Virginia War Museum
9285 Warwick Boulevard
Newport News, VA 23607
Telephone: 757-928-6738
Website: www.warmuseum.org

Private Collections

Many wonderful artifacts and books belong to private collectors. You will need to network to find these sources. Networking can be accomplished in an effective manner by attending Civil War trade shows and asking different collectors if they have anything or know where you can obtain information on the topics you seek. Running ads in Civil War publications may also elicit replies by individuals willing to help you.

Town Records

Each county has a courthouse where such vital statistics as births, deaths, marriages, divorces, land transactions, and deeds are recorded. These can be very informative, especially when doing genealogy work to trace an ancestor, or to see the old maps to put battles into perspective, etc. County clerks and abstractors are often gold mines of information.

Church Records

Many churches and religious institutions maintain records that are helpful for genealogical research. The Mormon Church in particular maintains amazing repositories of genealogical information about people of all denominations.

Genealogical Records

Local, regional, and national genealogical societies also may be able to help you in your search, especially if you are seeking personal information on an ancestor.

If you're seeking genealogical societies, a starting point is the National Genealogical Society, 4527 17th Street North, Arlington, VA 22207. Telephone: 703-525-0050. Website: http://www.ngsgenealogy.org. The NGS has several publications available for purchase, as well as some very helpful brochures with basic information on getting started.

The Church of Jesus Christ of Latter Day Saints (the Mormons) has maintained an active microfilming program designed to collect genealogical material from all over the United States. It may be helpful in your quest to contact the Genealogical Society, 58 East North Temple Street, Salt Lake City, UT 84150. Telephone: 801-538-2978. The society also maintains branches throughout the United States. Call the main headquarters to find the nearest location.

Census Records

The 1890 Census. Although this research aid is often used, many researchers overlook its existence. The 11th census of the United States included a special census of Union Civil War veterans. This form included columns for the name of surviving soldiers, sailors, and marines, and widows; rank; company; name of regiment or vessel; date of enlistment; date of discharge; length of service; post office address; disability incurred; and remarks. Unfortunately, most of this census was destroyed in a fire, and the surviving section only includes part of Kentucky through Washington, alphabetically.

Civil War Battlefield Sites

Civil War battlefield parks also maintain research libraries with book and manuscript collections. Before visiting any of the park libraries, call ahead to schedule an appointment. Most sites have limited facilities for researchers and need to know when you're coming so they can prepare and reserve space for you. Many other sites are in state and local hands.

The current Civil War sites maintained by the National Park Service include:

Andersonville National Historic Site
Route 1   Box 85
Andersonville, GA 31711
Telephone: 912-924-0343
Website: www.nps.gov/ande

Antietam National Battlefield
P.O. Box 158
Sharpsburg, MD 21782
Telephone: 301-432-5124
Website: www.nps.gov/anti

Appomattox Court House National Historic Park
P.O. Box 218
Appomattox, VA 24522
Telephone: 804-352-8987
Website: www.nps.gov/apco

Brice's Cross Roads National Battlefield Site
c/o Natchez Trace Parkway
2680 Nanchez Trace Parkway
Tupelo, MS 38804
Telephone: 601-680-4025
Website: www.nps.gov/brcr

Chickamauga and Chattanooga National Military Park
P.O. Box 2128
Fort Oglethorpe, GA 30742
Telephone: 706-866-9241
Website: www.nps.gov/chch

Fort Donelson National Battlefield
P.O. Box 434
Dover, TN 37058
Telephone: 931-232-5706 or 931-232-5348
Website: www.nps.gov/fodo

Fort Jefferson National Monument
c/o Dry Tortugas National Park
P.O. Box 6208
Key West, FL 33041
Telephone: 305-242-7700
Website: www.nps.gov/drto

Fort Pulaski National Monument
P.O. Box 30757
Savannah, GA 31410
Telephone: 912-786-5787
Website: www.nps.gov/fopu

Fort Sumter National Monument
1214 Middle Street
Sullivan's Island SC 29482
Telephone: 843-883-3123
Website: www.nps.gov/fosu

Fredericksburg and Spotsylvania National Military Park
120 Chatham Lane
Fredericksburg, VA 22405
Telephone: 540-373-6122
Website: www.nps.gov/frsp

Gettysburg National Military Park
97 Taneytown Road
Gettysburg, PA 17325
Telephone: 717-334-1124
Website: www.nps.gov/gett

Glorietta Unit
Pecos National Historical Park
P.O. Box 418
Pecos, NM 87552
Telephone: 505-757-6414
Website: www.nps.gov/peco

Harpers Ferry National Historical Park
P.O. Box 65
Harpers Ferry, WV 25425
Telephone: 304-535-6223
Website: www.nps.gov/hafe

Kennesaw Mountain National Battlefield Park
900 Kennesaw Mountain Drive
Kennesaw, GA 30144
Telephone: 770-427-4686 x225
Website: www.nps.gov/kemo

Manassas National Battlefield Park
6511 Sudley Road
Manassas, VA 22110
Telephone: 703-361-1339
Website: www.nps.gov/mana

Monocacy National Battlefield
4801 Urbana Pike
Frederick, MD 21704
Telephone: 301-662-3515
Website: www.nps.gov/mono

Pea Ridge National Military Park
P.O. Box 700
Pea Ridge, AR 72751
Telephone: 501-451-8122
Website: www.nps.gov/peri

Petersburg National Battlefield
1539 Hickory Hill Road
Petersburg, VA 23803
Telephone: 804-732-3531
Website: www.nps.gov/pete

Richmond National Battlefield Park
3215 East Broad Street
Richmond, VA 23223
Telephone: 804-226-1981
Website: www.nps.gov/rich

Shiloh National Military Park
1055 Pittsburg Landing Road
Shiloh, TN 38376
Telephone: 901-689-5275
Website: www.nps.gov/shil

Stones River National Battlefield
3501 Old Nashville Highway
Murfreesboro, TN 37129
Telephone: 615-893-9501
Website: www.nps.gov/stri

Tupelo National Battlefield
c/o Natchez Trace Parkway
2680 Natchez Trace Parkway
Tupelo, MS 38804
Telephone: 662-680-4025
Website: www.nps.gov/tupe

Vicksburg National Military Park
3201 Clay Street
Vicksburg, MS 39183
Telephone: 601-636-0583
Website: www.nps.gov/vick

Wilsons Creek National Battlefield
6424 West Farm Road
Republic, MO 65738
Telephone: 417-732-2662
Website: www.nps.gov/wicr

Many other battlefield and historic sites are in the custody of individual states or other organizations. Examples are Pamplin Park in Virginia, Olustee in Florida, Perryville in Kentucky, and Forts Macon and Fisher in North Carolina.

For a comprehensive guide, see *The Civil War Trust's Official Guide to the Civil War Discovery Trail* (New York: Macmillan, 1996).

Trade Shows

Civil War trade shows can be invaluable sources of information. These shows last from one to three days, and bring together dealers of books, papers, artifacts, prints, and other Civil War-related material. Hundreds and thousands of people attend these shows in search of merchandise. By talking to dealers, you can sometimes find some who might have information or memorabilia you are looking for, or know of someone who collects relics on a topic of interest. *Civil War News* magazine and *Civil War Courier* magazine list dates and places of shows.

The Internet

Many people are finding great sources of information on the Civil War from the Internet, electronic bulletin boards, and discussion groups. Most large public libraries and university libraries, including the Library of Congress, have placed their card catalogs on the Internet. This is a handy way of checking the availability of books. There are in addition thousands of Civil War sites and discussion groups where a researcher can get valuable information. Some of the major Civil War-related Web pages and discussion groups are as follows:

★ The United States Civil War Center
   http://www.cwc.lsu.edu

   This is the site to start your Civil War internet search. A review of books on the Civil War, links to researching people involved, national archives and state archival resources.

   attached: http://www.cwc.lsu.edu/cwc/civlink.htm#cwinfo

   A complete list of Civil War information, followed by Civil War resources, historic places included.

★ American Civil War Homepage
   http://sunsite.utk.edu/civil-war/warweb.html

   Included is an outline of resources which develop into larger fields of study, such as general resources, documentary records, the secession crisis and before, histories, and bibliographies.

★ Civil War Biographies
   http://www.civilwarhome.com/biograph.htm

   This site displays biographies of some of the major people involved in the Civil War. Accompanied by images, and the person's contribution to the war.

★ Washington College Civil War Site
   http://www.janke.washcoll.edu/civilwar/civilwar.htm

   This is one of the best websites because it provides 50 categories of links to other Civil War sites, such as libraries and archives, book dealers, genealogy, Gettysburg, photographs, units, and more.

★ Library of Congress Homepage
   http://www.loc.gov

★ The Civil War in Georgia
   http://www.researchonline.net/gacw/mastindx.htm

   An index to Civil War soldiers, including their name, military unit, and company. The site explains each regiment, including organization and surrendering dates, officers, assignments, history, battles, rosters, and a bibliography for further research.

★ Time Line
http://www.californiacentralcoast.com/commun/map/civil/tl/timeline.html

A Civil War timeline, 1861-1865, and American Civil War exhibits, including a search for things not present, map exhibits, battles, and important people.

★ Civil War Sites on the Web
http://www.ugrr.org/civil/cw-web.htm

A large amount of Civil War resources, which can lead to dozens of links. For example, The Selected Civil War photographs collection, or Civil War battle summaries by state.

★ Rare Map Collection—The American Civil War
http://www.libs.uga.edu/darchive/hargrett/maps/civil.html

Tons of maps on the new world, colonial America, revolutionary America, Union and expansion.

★ The Civil War Archive—File Index
http://www.civilwararchive.com/files.htm

Includes regimental index, corps index, research room, roundtables, letters, diaries, and more.

★ Archives USA

This online system is a subscription service for libraries to access their comprehensive guide to archival sources. The service consists of three sections:

1. Listing of manuscript repositories that supersedes the older *Directory of Archival and Manuscript Repositories in the United States*

2. Records originally included in the *National Union Catalog of Manuscripts*, some 76,000 collections

3. *National Inventory of Documentary Sources in the United States*, an older microfiche series listing 44,000 collections.

For more information, the web page is:

http://archives.chadwyck.com/infopage/moreinfo.htm: or write to: Chadwyck-Healey, Inc., 1101 King Street, Alexandria, VA 22314, telephone 1-800-752-0515.

Newspapers

Civil War Newspapers

1860s newspapers are one of the most underused groups of potential information by both amateur and professional historians alike, primarily because there are few available indexes to help make research easier.

A hundred years ago, even the smallest towns usually had a weekly newspaper so the local people could obtain local, national, and international news. Since most folks did not travel very far from their homes for any length of time, towns and families maintained strong ties to each other. When the war broke out, it was the first time that many of the young men on both sides were away from home for an extended period of time. It was an exciting, if dangerous, time in their lives, and the soldiers wished to share their travails with the folks back home.

As a result, many regiments had unofficial correspondents who sent letters to their hometown newspapers. The papers would then print these letters so the folks could read about what the local soldiers were doing. Unlike the two world wars in which Americans served, Civil War soldiers did not have their mail censored and were free to write about anything and everything they did and saw. It was no joke that General Lee said that the best source of information about the enemy was obtained by reading Northern newspapers.

Thus, many Civil War-period newspapers are chock full of soldier letters and other kernels of information such as casualty lists and tidbits about local men in uniform. For example, I have examined more than 100 Pennsylvania newspapers in search of Civil War information, and have located more than 7,700 letters

from soldiers in the field. And not just Pennsylvania soldiers, but men from several other states as well. Many letters were terse and devoid of important military information, but hundreds were a researcher's dream—detailed descriptions of battles, marches, and camp life.

On the Confederate homefront, although more than 800 newspapers were published during the war, few had large circulations and only 10 percent were dailies. Many papers were discontinued or forced to move as a result of advancing Union armies. Still, quite a number of issues have survived and are treasure troves of information.

Dozens of soldier-operated newspapers, both North and South, were also published during the war. Some were run out of captured local newspaper offices as Union armies moved south, while a few were handwritten in prisons and hospitals. Popular features included military humor, political propaganda, provost marshal regulations, and health care advice from surgeons.

To find out what newspapers were published in the 1860s, contact your local library for help. The standard guide is:

📖 Winifred Gregory, *American Newspapers, 1821-1936*. NY: H. W. Wilson, 1937; reprint edition, NY: Kraus Publications, 1967.

Gregory's guide includes a listing of papers then held by over 5700 repositories.

Also useful, and overlooked, is:

📖 Simon N. D. North, *History and Present Condition of the Periodical Press of the United States*. Washington: Government Printing Office, 1884.

Simon included a study of American newspapers from 1639 to 1880. His Appendix D listed the bound files of newspapers owned by the American Antiquarian Society in Worcester, MA. The Society is, today, the second largest repository of newspaper titles in America after the Library of Congress.

The University of Texas at Austin maintains a special collections library:

🏛 The Center for American History
Sid Richardson Hall 2.101
Austin, TX 78712
Telephone: 512-495-4515
Website: www.lib.utexas.edu/Libs/CAH

The Southern Newspaper Collection (1790-1900) contains newspapers published in every state of the former Confederacy.

★ Accessible Archives, Inc. (697 Sugartown Road, Malvern, PA 19355; Telephone: 610-296-7441; Website: www.accessible.com) has published "The Civil War: A Newspaper Perspective," a database in CD-ROM format and on their website by subscription, that includes the contents of three newspapers—*New York Herald, Charleston Mercury, Richmond Enquirer*—for the period from November 1, 1860, through April 30, 1865. This publication includes more than 11,000 articles and 700 maps and illustrations.

If your local library does not have any collection of newspapers, contact your local historical society or college library. Finally, your state library or archives will probably have a sizeable collection of Civil War newspapers, originals or microfilm copies, for you to browse through in search of information. Such work is often tedious, occasionally inspiring, and always interesting, because you never know what you will find.

The following books will be very helpful to your newspaper research:

📖 J. Cutler Andrews, *The North Reports the Civil War* (1955, reprinted 1985).

📖 J. Cutler Andrews, *The South Reports the Civil War* (1970, reprinted 1985).

For an overview of Civil War newspapers and reporters

📖 David Bosse, *Civil War Newspaper Maps: An Historical Atlas.* Baltimore: Johns Hopkins University Press, 1993.

Provides an excellent bibliography of Civil War newspaper studies.

The Illustrated Newspapers of the War Period

In addition to the daily and weekly newspapers circulated locally, several papers printed weekly editions that were read nationwide. Three papers published in New York dominated the Northern market—*Harper's Weekly, Frank Leslie's Illustrated Newspaper,* and the *New York Illustrated News.* Each of these papers was filled with war news as well as illustrations produced by a host of special artists hired to sketch the war. These men included Alfred Waud, Thomas Nast, James E. Taylor, Winslow Homer, Edwin Forbes, Theodore R. Davis, and several other talented men.

HarpWeek has made available for purchase to libraries and other institutions through the internet a website containing indexes and the scanned pages of *Harper's Weekly* in the Civil War era. Check with your local or university libraries to see if they have purchased this access. (Website is www.harpweek.com)

Currently Bell & Howell Information and Learning and Harper's Magazine Foundation are collaborating to produce *Harper's Magazine Online.* The first installation due in spring of 2000 will contain indexing from 1850 to 1877. Access will be available to individuals by subscription. For more information check Chadwyck-Healey's website at www.chadwyck.com.

On the Southern homefront, the *Southern Illustrated News,* published in Richmond from 1863-1865, was a source of information, but the most sketches of the Southern war effort were published in the *Illustrated London News,* which hired correspondent Frank Vizetelly to cover the conflict.

Postwar Newspapers

Throughout the later 19th and early 20th centuries, many local newspapers printed articles by, or recollections of, veterans. Again, because of the lack of good newspaper indexes, it is difficult to locate these articles; however, if you have the persistence to dig through local newspapers, you may find lots of unused gems waiting to be rediscovered.

My own experience has been quite gratifying because of the discoveries

> ★—Research Tip—★
> If you find scrapbooks of newspaper clippings in Civil War-related collections, don't hesitate to carefully review them. You're likely to find that some veterans cut out clippings relating to their units or favorite battles and assembled them for easier reading. At times, though, they failed to note the paper and dates of issue they got these articles from.

I've made. For example, Bates Alexander of the 7th Pennsylvania Reserves published his recollections in the *Hummelstown Sun* in the 1890s; his battle descriptions are among the best that I've ever read. Likewise, James M. Linn of the 51st Pennsylvania was a regular contributor to one of his hometown newspapers, the *Lewisburg Chronicle.*

Some newspapers featured Civil War columns that ran regularly and attracted a wide reading audience. Two deserve a brief mention here because of their importance. Alexander K. McClure, editor of the *Philadelphia Times,* started a weekly version of the paper in 1877 built around the "Annals of the War" column that he started. McClure solicited reminiscences from Union and Confederate veterans alike. In 1879, his company published the 800-page *The Annals of the War, Written by Leading Participants North and South,* which included most of the articles printed since the column's inception. However, most researchers don't realize that the "Annals of the War" column ran on into the late 1880s until it finally petered out, having included more than 800 articles from hundreds of veterans.

One of McClure's competitors, Isaac R. Pennypacker, started a "Pennsylvania in the War" column in the *Philadelphia Weekly Press.* This series ran from 1886-1889 and featured articles from notables such as John F. Hartranft, Lafayette McLaws, Samuel W. Crawford, Alfred Pleasonton, John Gibbon, Evander M. Law, James W. Latta, and other important officers.

Postwar Veterans' Publications

As Union army veterans joined the Grand Army of the Republic organization and became politically active, they also published a wide range of magazines and newspapers. Not all have survived in quantity, but a number of these publications are extremely useful for Civil War historical research. All of these volumes contain articles of historical importance, obituaries, and general news of interest to veterans. They include:

📖 The National Tribune

George E. Lemon, a wounded veteran and expert pension lawyer, started this monthly newspaper in 1877 as an aid for soldiers seeking pensions from the government. He gradually accepted historical articles for inclusion, and in August 1881 the National Tribune *became a weekly newspaper of 8 or 12 pages. Contributors of historical articles and letters ranged from privates to generals such as Green B. Raum, Oliver O. Howard, William P. Carlin, and John Pope.*

The Tribune is perhaps the greatest source of little-used Civil War information available. The paper is still being published as the Stars and Stripes National Tribune.

This author has written a series of guide-indexes to the Tribune *entitled* "To Care For Him Who Has Borne the Battle": Research Guide to Civil War Material in the National Tribune. *Volume 1: 1877-1884, is currently available. Subsequent volumes will be forthcoming, including subject indexes.*

📖 American Tribune

Published in Indianapolis from 1880 through 1906, this was another veterans' paper although not as successful as the National Tribune.

📖 Grand Army Scout and Soldiers Mail

Published in Philadelphia during the 1880s, this weekly magazine also printed historical articles of interest to modern researchers.

📖 Grand Army Record

This was published in Boston from 1885 to 1900.

Confederate veterans published the following:

📖 Confederate Veteran

40 volumes published in Nashville between 1893 and 1932. This valuable set has been reprinted with a 3-volume index by Broadfoot Publishing Company (1993).

📖 Our Living and Our Dead

This was published in Raleigh by the North Carolina branch of the Southern Historical Society, in 4 volumes (1874-1876).

📖 Southern Bivouac: A Monthly Literary and Historical Magazine

Five volumes from 1882-1887, also reprinted and indexed by Broadfoot Publishing Company.

📖 Southern Historical Society Papers

52 volumes from 1876 to 1959. An invaluable source for Civil War history. Includes reports, correspondence, letters, and contributions from privates to generals. Broadfoot Publishing Company has reprinted the entire set (1977) and provided a cumulative index (1980). Morningside Press has also reprinted the set and provided a name index (Kate Pleasants Minor, Southern Historical Society Papers Index (Dayton: Press of Morningside, 1970, 1978).

Magazines, Journals, and Newsletters

Some current Civil War publications that may contain articles of relevance to your research include the following:

📖 *America's Civil War*
741 Miller Drive SE
Suite D-2
Leesburg, VA 22075
Telephone: 703-771-9400; subscriptions: 800-435-9610
Website: historynet.com

A popular bimonthly magazine that features a wide array of articles about battles, leaders, and other Civil War topics.

📖 *Blue & Gray Magazine*
P.O. Box 28685
522 Norton Road
Columbus, OH 43228
Telephone: 614-870-1861, or 800-CIVIL-WAR
Website: www.bluegraymagazine.com

A bimonthly magazine that features tours of Civil War sites together with authoritative articles on the war, book reviews, and a current events column. The magazine also has a mail order book catalog available upon request and offers back issues and reprints.

📖 *Camp Chase Gazette*
P.O. Box *707*
Marietta, OH 45750
Telephone: 740-373-1865
Website: www.campchase.com

This magazine is published 10 times per year for reenactors, and includes articles of interest as well as national schedules of events and advertisements from suppliers. The magazine also offers a free classified ad to subscribers.

📖 *Civil War Courier*
2507 Delaware Avenue
Buffalo, NY 14216
Telephone: 800-418-1861 or 716-873-2594\
Website: www.civilwarcourier.com

A newspaper publication which appears 10 times per year and includes articles and book reviews as well as buy-sell-trade-information classified ads. It also includes a calendar of events and prints reader requests for information.

📖 *Civil War History*
Kent State University Press
Kent, OH 44242
Telephone: 330-672-7913

This quarterly journal publishes scholarly, footnoted articles about the Civil War era. Includes in-depth book reviews.

☐ *The Civil War Lady Magazine*
622 Third Avenue SW
Pipestone, MN 56164
Telephone: 515-228-1861

A bimonthly magazine devoted to reenactors portraying women of the period, with articles on clothing, etiquette, fashion, social history, photographs, reenacting supplies. Sponsors an annual conference.

☐ *Civil War News*
234 Monarch Hill Road
Tunbridge, VT 05077
Telephone: 800-777-1862
Website: www.civilwarnews.com

This leading newspaper-format magazine covers reenacting, battlefield preservation, and other news of interest to Civil War buffs, including book reviews, classified ads, and an events calendar. Published 11 times per year.

☐ *Civil War Regiments*
Savas Publishing Company
202 First Street SE
Suite 103A
Mason City, IA 50401
Telephone: 515-421-7135
Website: www.savaspublishing.com

A quarterly journal with documented studies of Civil War units, North and South, with book reviews and other articles on command, strategy, and tactics.

📖 *Civil War Times Illustrated*
6405 Flank Drive
Harrisburg, PA 17112
Telephone: 717-657-9555
Website: www.civilwartimes.com

The Civil War magazine with the largest circulation, publishing articles covering the entire spectrum of the Civil War period. Written in a popular style and published bimonthly.

📖 *Columbiad*
741 Miller Drive SE, Suite D-2
Leesburg, VA 20175
Orders: 1-800-829-3340

A *quarterly journal sponsored by* Civil War Times Illustrated.

📖 *The Gettysburg Magazine*
Morningside Bookshop
260 Oak Street
Dayton, OH 45410
Telephone: 800-648-9710
Website: www.morningsidebooks.com

Strictly about the campaign and battle of Gettysburg, with footnoted, scholarly articles. Published in January and July.

📖 *Journal of Confederate History Book Series*
Southern Heritage Press
4035 Emerald Drive
Murfreesboro, TN 37130
Telephone: 615-895-5642

Originally in magazine format, this is now a series of books published about Confederate history.

📖 *Lincoln Herald*
Lincoln Memorial University
Harrogate, TN 37752
Telephone: 423-869-6235

A quarterly journal devoted to Abraham Lincoln, but also publishes general Civil War articles.

📖 *Military Images*
RR 2, Box 99-A
Lesoine Drive
Henryville, PA 18332
Website: www.civilwar-photos.com

A photographic magazine published six times a year featuring the American military of the nineteenth century, with heavy emphasis on the Civil War.

📖 *Museum of the Confederacy Journal*
1201 East Clay Street
Richmond, VA 23219
Telephone: 804-649-1861
Website: www.moc.org

A well-illustrated journal with articles based on the museum's fine collections of Civil War artifacts.

📖 *North & South*
P.O. Box 1027
Escondido, CA 92033
Telephone: 800-546-6707
Website: www.northandsouthmagazine.com

This magazine began publishing in late 1997, with 7 issues each year. The owner's aim is to produce a scholarly magazine with fresh research.

📖 *North South Trader's Civil War*
P.O. Drawer 631
Orange, VA 22960
Telephone: 540-672-4845

Magazine devoted to artifacts and history, with articles covering both subjects.

📖 *Southern Partisan*
   1620 Gervais Street
   Columbia, SC 29201
   Telephone: 800-264-2559

   *A magazine devoted to the Southern cause, including histori-
   cal articles and news of current events.*

📖 *Trans-Mississippi News*
   Camp Pope Bookshop
   P.O. Box 2232
   Iowa City, IA 52244
   Telephone: 800-204-2407

   *Quarterly newsletter with articles, book reviews, preservation
   news, events.*

Organizing
Your
Information

As you proceed in your research, you will gather much information, in the form of notes, copies, key phone numbers, helpful people, etc. There are several ways to organize your information:

★ In file folders, by category. Be generous with the file folders, subdividing into manageable packets of data. Since you will probably need a lot of file folders, look for a discount office supply store or other discount store. File folders can be stored in portable plastic file holders, cardboard file boxes, file cabinets, or on a shelf with a bookend to hold them upright. Remember, folders don't work unless you keep material in them!

★ On note cards. This is the time honored method for bibliographies and other types of research where the data can fit onto one or both sides of a single index card. You may choose from a variety of sizes, from 3x5 to 5x8 or larger. File boxes are available in many sizes and styles, and are very portable. For additional organizing, you can use dividers or colored note cards.

★ In notebooks, with a separate color-tabbed section for each topic.

★ By computer. For this, you will need a computer with a good amount of available hard memory, a good word-processing program such as WordPerfect or Microsoft Word, and backup floppy disks. Also, hitting the wrong button can erase hours of work, so backing it up onto paper or another disk is very important.

★ Making piles on the floor or bookcase. This is very popular for certain phases of research and for certain topics, but lacks portability and may aggravate others in your household.

★ Any combination of these methods.

The important thing to remember is to choose a method you are familiar with, that you can and will use, so that you can find your data when you need it and not waste hours looking for things. Also, certain types of research will lend themselves more naturally to one method or another. Being organized is a very important part of doing research effectively.

5

Writing

There are several issues to consider when you begin to pull your research together into a coherent unified product. These issues include:

★ Purpose and goals
★ Style
★ Documentation
★ Footnotes/Endnotes
★ Indexing
★ Method of writing
★ Permission to publish
★ Submitting your work

Purpose and Goals

The amount and nature of your writing will be determined by your goal. I encourage you to set down your thoughts on paper; your thoughts will change as your focus changes. If you have been researching a relative, you will want to put your information together as part of a family history, so that subsequent generations can read your findings as a coherent story. This can be done as a narrative, or in outline form. There are excellent workbooks and computer programs on the market for organizing family/genealogical history.

On the other hand, if you are going to write a magazine article on your topic, you need to review each magazine's rules for submission, recommended length of articles, preferred style (to be discussed later), etc. If possible, it's a good idea to make some calls to the editors of the various magazines to see if they are interested in the topic.

If you are going to be writing a full-length book, you will need to group your material into categories, and then into chapters. Making an outline will also help with preparing a table of contents. As regards length of book, initially just let it flow; write as much as you can or want to. You can always pare it down later or look for more data if necessary.

A good source for general information on how to write, as well as how to sell your manuscript, is contained in *The Writer's Handbook* (annual editions published by The Writer, Inc., Boston). This handy guide is available in most bookstores.

Style

To keep things simple, read one of the general style manuals and stick to one style when you write and record your notes. I recommend *The Chicago Manual of Style*, 14th edition (University of Chicago Press, 1993) for bibliographic and footnote styles. Other style manuals are published by the Modern Language Association (*MLA Handbook for Writers of Research Papers*, 4th edition, NY, 1995; and *The MLA Style Manual*, 6th printing, NY, 1985), and the *U.S. Government Printing Office's Style Manual* (28th edition), among many others of lesser importance. Books and articles to be published will need proper footnotes and bibliography to be taken seriously. Fiction works do not generally require such strict style, but a brief bibliography for further reading might be a good idea.

Documentation

When you're writing about history, you must cite your sources and include notes detailed enough so other researchers can use your material in the future. Remember, history is different for everyone, and researchers often have different goals in mind when writing about a favorite subject. Interpretation of the same document can be varied, so leave a proper trail so others can use the sources you cited.

Always save your notes, even when you've finished a manuscript and are searching for a publisher. If you're ever questioned about a source or an editor asks you to rewrite a section to clarify something, then your original notes are invaluable. It is also not uncommon to get calls or letters from researchers for years, asking for more specifics, more references, or where you found a particular document.

Footnotes and Endnotes

In historical writing, the prime source of documentation is the footnote or endnote. Most books use endnotes, placed after the main text in order of appearance. Some publishers use footnotes, placing these notes at the bottom of the same page where the text occurs.

★—Tip—★
You can group your sources for each paragraph into one note, using semicolons to separate each source.

There are several style guides that include detailed information on footnotes. Most historians use *The Chicago Manual of Style.* A condensed version is Kate L. Turabian, *A Manual for Writers of Term Papers, Theses and Dissertations,* 5th edition (Chicago: University of Chicago Press, 1987).

Footnotes/endnotes are used to document your sources and can be used by other researchers to review the information you gathered while doing their own research. Thus, when documenting your work, you should be as thorough as possible.

★—Tip—★
For further information and more examples, consult Turabian or The Chicago Manual of Style. Look at scholarly books and articles and read through the footnotes to see readily-available examples.

In most writing, you need only to place one footnote/endnote number after each paragraph, unless you quote directly from more than one source; to avoid confusion, use a separate note for each quotation.

Generally, keep in mind that you need to identify the sources of your information well enough so that others can find the documents you cited to write your material.

★ Published material cited should include the author's name, title of the work, place of publication, publisher, date, and page number(s), as follows:

John Q. Imholte. *The First Volunteers: History of the First Minnesota Volunteer Regiment, 1861-1865.* (Minneapolis: Ross and Haines, Inc., 1963), 37-38.

Subsequent citations can appear as:
Imholte, *First Minnesota,* 41.

★ Journal articles should include the author's name, title of article, name of journal, volume number, year, and page number(s):

John Purifoy, "The Captured Dispatches," *Confederate Veteran 32* (1941): 390-91.

Subsequent citations can appear as:
Purifoy, "Captured Dispatches," 392.

★ Record Groups in the National Archives (as well as similar citations), use the following approach:

William S. Bennett to Henry L. Stimson, September 6, 1911, Gettysburg Battlefield Commission Papers, Records of the Office of the Quartermaster General, Record Group 92, National Archives.

Subsequent citations can appear as:
Bennett to Stimson, September 6, 1911, RG 92.

Indexing

You will please an editor's heart, and ultimately the reader's, if you take the time and care to prepare an index.

For the fundamentals about indexing and converting a book's text into "keys to the substance in the index," see Virginia S. Thatcher, *Indexes* (Lanham, MD: Scarecrow Press, 1995). *The Chicago Manual of Style* also has a lengthy section on indexing.

If you need further help in indexing, there are a number of firms that specialize in indexing. For a list, see *Literary Market Place: The Directory of the American Book Publishing Industry* (New Providence, NJ: R. R. Bowker, 1997).

✍ Do not compile a final index until the publisher sends you page proofs to review for errors. Your book is then set in final form so you can safely compile the index without worrying about any changes in page numbers.

Permission to Publish

Permission is required any time you quote extensively from a source, published or unpublished. If it is a **published work,** you will need to get permission from the publisher. If it is an **unpublished document**, you will need to get permission from the library or repository, and if you need to go back to the **original donors** of the material, the library will advise you on how to proceed. The same rules apply to publishing **photographs and illustrations**. You also need to mention the credit for permission to publish in the work itself, generally in the acknowledgments or in the caption below the photograph. Occasionally this information will appear on the copyright page. Also, remember that to protect yourself legally, always obtain written permission to publish.

Method of Writing

The exact method is up to you. Some people use a computer word-processing program, some type it out longhand, some handwrite and then type, etc. I even know of one writer of historical fiction who uses a quill pen, ink, and old-time heavyweight paper, and writes in a room with no modern items to distract her.

The plus side of using a computer is that it is easy to make corrections without retyping the entire document; you can cut and paste easily and move whole chunks of data around, and most machines have a spell-check function. Most publishers accept manuscripts on disk (but never send your original disk; send a copy); always check with the publisher first to make sure your disk is compatible with their system.

The Decision to Publish

The decision to publish is an important one, not to be taken lightly. The most recent estimates I've seen are that only 10 percent of manuscripts get published. There is a lot of competition out there, and many publishers' budgets are limited. You may need to shop your manuscript around a bit to find a publisher; patience and persistence are key.

Another important consideration is that you should always make more than one copy of your manuscript. It is truly amazing how often people make only one copy of their work and then lose it. If you use a computer, make a backup diskette as well as a paper copy for reference purposes. When sending out your manuscript to a publisher, send a copy (including illustrations) and keep the original. Do not send original photographs. There are some publishers out there who will give you a hard time about getting your photos back if they reject your manuscript.

Remember too that even if a publisher rejects your manuscript, it is not a rejection of you as a person, even though it sure may feel like it, after all the hard work you put into your manuscript. Read the comments the publisher sends back (most publishers send out manuscripts to readers/consultants for opinions regarding accuracy, general appeal, publishability, etc.) Make the necessary corrections unless they are totally outrageous or inappropriate. Have faith that eventually you will be published. Try again, submitting a clean copy of your manuscript to a different press. Do not send a dog-eared, marked up copy that you got back from another publisher; it will not present your material in the best possible light.

A visit to your local library will let you locate books about publishing. A current popular text is Ted Nicholas, *How to Publish a Book* (Chicago, IL: Enterprise-Dearborn).

Publications Checklist

Here is a suggested working checklist to consider when preparing to submit your manuscript for peer review or to an editor or publisher:

1. Title
2. Sub-Title
3. Title Page Format
4. Dedication
5. Table of Contents
6. List of Illustrations/Maps
7. Preface/Forward
8. Acknowledgments/Credits
9. Note on Style
10. Introduction
11. Chapter Headings/Arrangements
12. Text
13. Footnotes/Endnotes
14. Bibliography/Essay on Sources
15. Illustration Credits
16. Index

> **Remember to be patient, persistent, and creative in your approach and to explore all possible sources of information. Ask for help when you need it. Above all, enjoy the thrill of finding the information you seek, and be on the lookout for "hidden treasures" that may not be what you are looking for now but may come in handy later.**

APPENDIX

LIST OF STATE ARCHIVES, LIBRARIES, AND HISTORICAL SOCIETIES

★ ALABAMA
Alabama Department of Archives and History
624 Washington Avenue
Montgomery, AL 36103
Telephone: 334-242-4363

★ ALASKA
Alaska State Archives and Records Management Services
141 Willoughby Avenue
Juneau, AK 99811
Telephone: 907-465-2270
Website: www.eed.state.ak.us/lam/archives

Alaska State Library
P.O. Box 110571
Juneau, AK 99811
Telephone: 907-465-2910
Website: www.eed.state.ak.us/lam/library

★ ARIZONA

Arizona State Archives
1700 West Washington
Phoenix, AZ 85007
Telephone: 602-542-4159
Website: www.dlapr.lib.az.us

Arizona State Library
State Capitol
Room 200, 1700 West Washington
Phoenix, AZ 85007
Telephone: 602-542-4035

★ ARKANSAS

Arkansas History Commission
One Capitol Mall
Little Rock, AR 72201
Telephone: 501-682-6900
Website: www.state.ar.us/ahc/ahc.html

Arkansas State Library
One Capitol Mall, 5th Floor
Little Rock, AR 72201
Telephone: 501-682-1527

★ CALIFORNIA

California State Archives
1020 O Street
Sacramento, CA 95814
Telephone: 916-653-7715

California State Library
914 Capitol Mall, P.O. Box 942837
Sacramento, CA 94237
Telephone: 916-654-0183
Website: www.library.ca.gov

★ COLORADO
Colorado Division of State Archives and Public Records
1313 Sherman Street, Room 1-B20
Denver, CO 80203
Telephone: 303-866-2055 or 2390
Website: www.archives.state.co.us

Colorado Historical Society
1300 Broadway
Denver, CO 802203
Telephone: 303-866-2305
Website: www.coloradohistory.org

Colorado State Library
201 East Colfax Avenue, Room 309
Denver, CO 80203
Telephone: 303-866-6900

★ CONNECTICUT
Connecticut Adjutant General
Records Officer, State Armory
360 Broad Street
Hartford, CT 06115

Connecticut State Library
231 Capitol Avenue
Hartford, CT 06106
Telephone: 860-566-4777

Connecticut Historical Society
One Elizabeth Street
Hartford, CT 06105
Telephone: 860-236-5621
Website: www.chs.org

★ DELAWARE
Delaware State Archives, Hall of Records
121 Duke of York Street
Dover, DE 19901
Telephone: 302-739-5318

Historical Society of Delaware
505 North Market Street Mall
Wilmington, DE 19801
Telephone: 302-655-7161
Website: www.hsd.org

Delaware State Library
43 South Dupont Highway
Dover, DE 19901
Telephone: 302-739-4748

★ FLORIDA
Florida Bureau of Archives and Records Management
R. A. Gray Building
500 South Bronough Street

Tallahassee, FL 32399
Telephone: 850-487-2073
Website: http://dlis.dos.state.fl.us/barm

Florida State Library
same address
Telephone: 850-487-2651

★ GEORGIA
Department of Archives and History
Civil War Records Section
330 Capitol Avenue SE
Atlanta, GA 30334
Telephone: 404-656-2350

★ HAWAII
Hawaii State Archives
Iolani Palace Grounds
Honolulu, HA 96813
Telephone:808-586-0329

Hawaiian Historical Society
560 Kawaiahao Street
Honolulu, HA 96813
Telephone: 808-537-6271
Website: www.hawaiianhistory.org

★ IDAHO
Idaho State Historical Society Library and Archives
450 North 4th Street
Boise, ID 83702
Telephone: 208-334-3356

Idaho State Library
325 West State Street
Boise, ID 83702
Telephone: 208-334-2150

★ ILLINOIS

Illinois State Archives
Archives Building, Capitol Complex
Springfield, IL 62756
Telephone: 217-782-4682
Website: www.sos.state.il.us

Illinois State Historical Library
Old State Capitol Building
Springfield, IL 62701
Telephone: 217-524-6358

Illinois State Library
300 South 2nd Street
Springfield, IL 72601
Telephone: 217-785-5600

Illinois State Historical Society
210½ South 6th Street
Suite 200
Springfield, IL 62701
Telephone: 217-525-2781
Website: www.prairienet.org/ishs

★ INDIANA

   Indiana State Archives
   140 North Senate Avenue, Room 117
   Indianapolis, IN 46204
   Telephone: 317-232-3660

   Indiana State Library
   same address
   Telephone: 317-232-3675

   Indiana Historical Society Library
   450 West Ohio Street
   Indianapolis, IN 46202
   Telephone: 317-232-1879
   Website: www.indianahistory.org

★ IOWA

   State Historical Society of Iowa
   600 East Locust
   Des Moines, IA 50319
   Telephone: 515-281-6200
   Website: www.culturalaffairs.org/shsi/index.html

   Iowa State Library
   East 12th and Grand
   Des Moines, IA 50319
   Telephone: 515-281-4105

★ KANSAS

Kansas State Historical Society
6425 SW 6th Street
Topeka, KS 66615
Telephone: 785-272-8681
Website: www.kshs.org

Kansas State Library
State Capitol Building
300 Southwest 10th Avenue
Room 343 North
Topeka, KS 66612
Telephone: 785-296-3296

★ KENTUCKY

Kentucky Department for Libraries and Archives
300 Coffee Tree Road
Frankfort, KY 40602
Telephone: 502-564-8300

Kentucky Historical Society
100 West Broadway
Frankfort, KY 40601
Telephone: 502-564-3016
Website: www.kentuckyhistory.org

★ LOUISIANA

Louisiana Division of Archives
Records Management and History
3851 Essen Lane
P.O. Box 94125
Baton Rouge, LA 70804

Telephone: 225-922-1207
Website: www.sec.state.la.us

Louisiana State Library
701 North 4th Street
Baton Rouge, LA 70821
Telephone: 225-342-4913

★ MAINE

Maine State Archives
Cultural Building
State House Station 84
Augusta, ME 04333
Telephone: 207-287-5795

Maine State Library
Cultural Building
State House Station 64
Augusta, ME 04333
Telephone: 207-287-5600

★ MARYLAND

Maryland State Archives
350 Rowe Boulevard
Annapolis, MD 21401
Telephone: 410-260-6400
Website: www.mdarchives.state.md.us

★ MASSACHUSETTS

Massachusetts State Archives, Columbia Point
220 Morrissey Boulevard
Boston, MA 02125
Telephone: 617-727-2816
Website: www.state.ma.us/sec/arc

Massachusetts Historical Society
1154 Boylston Street
Boston, MA 02215
Telephone: 617-536-1608
Website: www.masshist.org

★ MICHIGAN

Michigan State Archives
717 West Allegan Street
Lansing, MI 48918
Telephone: 517-373-1408
Website: www.sos.state.mi.us/history/archive/archive.html

Library of Michigan
same address
Telephone: 517-373-1580

★ MINNESOTA

Minnesota Historical Society
Division of Archives and Manuscripts
345 Kellogg Boulevard West
St. Paul, MN 55102
Telephone: 612-296-6126
Website: www.mnhs.org

★ MISSISSIPPI

Mississippi Department of Archives and History
P.O. Box 571
Jackson, MS 39205
Telephone: 601-359-6876

★ MISSOURI

State of Missouri Office of the Adjutant General
2302 Militia Drive
Jefferson City, MO 65101
Telephone 314-526-9500

Missouri Historical Society and Archives
Jefferson Memorial Building
Forest Park, P.O. Box 11940
St. Louis, MO 63112
Telephone: 314-746-4500
Website: mohistory.org

★ MONTANA

Montana Historical Society
Division of Archives and Manuscripts
225 North Roberts Street
Box 201201
Helena, MT 59620
Telephone: 406-444-2681
Website: www.his.state.mt.us

Montana State Library
1515 East 6th Street
P.O. Box 201800
Helena, MT 59620
Telephone: 406-444-3004
Website: www.msl.state.mt.us

★ NEBRASKA
Nebraska State Historical Society
State Archives Division
1500 R Street, P.O. Box 82554
Lincoln, NE 68501
Telephone: 402-471-4771
Website: www.nebraskahistory.org

★ NEVADA
Nevada State Library and Archives
Capitol Complex
100 North Stewart Street
Carson City, NV 89701
Telephone: 775-684-3360

★ NEW HAMPSHIRE
New Hampshire Division of Records and Archives
71 South Fruit Street
Concord, NH 03301
Telephone: 603-271-2236
Website: www.state.nh.us/state/archives.htm

New Hampshire Historical Society
30 Park Street
Concord, NH 03301
Telephone: 603-225-3381
Website: www.nhhistory.org

★ NEW JERSEY
New Jersey Department of State
Division of Archives and Records Management
185 West State Street, CN 307
Trenton, NJ 08625
Telephone: 609-292-6260

New Jersey State Library
CN520, 185 West State Street
Trenton, NJ 08625
Telephone: 609-292-6200

★ NEW MEXICO
New Mexico State Records Center and Archives
404 Montezuma
Santa Fe, NM 87503
Telephone: 505-827-8880

New Mexico State Library
325 Don Gaspar
Santa Fe, NM 85701
Telephone: 505-827-3800

★ NEW YORK

New York State Archives
Cultural Education Center
Empire State Plaza
Albany, NY 12230
Telephone: 518-474-8955
Website: sara.nysed.gov

New York State Library
same address
Telephone: 518-474-5930

★ NORTH CAROLINA

North Carolina State Archives
4614 Mail Service Center
Raleigh, NC 27699-4614
Telephone: 919-733-3952
Website: www.ah.dcr.state.nc.us

State Library of North Carolina
same address
Telephone: 919-733-2570

★ NORTH DAKOTA

State Historical Society of North Dakota
North Dakota Heritage Center
612 East Boulevard Avenue
Bismarck, ND 58505-0830
Telephone: 701-328-2666
Website: www.state.nd.us/hist

North Dakota State Library
Liberty Memorial Building
604 East Boulevard Avenue, Dept 250
Bismarck, ND 58505-0800
Telephone: 701-328-4622 or 1-800-472-2104
Website: www.ndsl.lib.state.nd.us

★ OHIO

Ohio Historical Society
1982 Velma Avenue
Columbus, OH 43211
Telephone: 614-297-2510
Website: www.ohiohistory.org

Ohio State Archives
1985 Velma Avenue
Columbus, OH 43211
Telephone: 614-466-1500

State Library of Ohio
65 South Front Street
Room 510
Columbus, OH 43215
Telephone: 614-644-6956

★ OKLAHOMA

Oklahoma Department of Libraries
Archives and Records Division
200 Northeast 18th Street
Oklahoma City, OK 73105
Telephone: 405-521-2502

Oklahoma Historical Society
2100 North Lincoln Blvd.
Oklahoma City, OK 73105
Telephone: 405-522-5209
Website: www.ok-history.mus.ok.us

★ OREGON

Oregon State Archives
800 Summer Street
Salem, OR 97310
Telephone: 503-373-0701
Website: http://arcweb.sos.state.or.us

Oregon Historical Society
1200 SW Park Avenue
Portland, OR 97205-2483
Telephone: 503-222-1741
Website: www.ohs.org

★ PENNSYLVANIA

Pennsylvania State Archives
P.O. Box 1026
Harrisburg, PA 17108
Telephone: 717-783-3281
Website: www.phmc.state.pa.us

State Library of Pennsylvania
Walnut Street and Commonwealth Avenue
P.O. Box 1601
Harrisburg, PA 17105
Telephone: 717-787-4440

★ RHODE ISLAND

Rhode Island State Archives
337 Westminster Street
Providence, RI 02903
Telephone: 401-222-2353
Website: http://archives.state.ri.us

Rhode Island State Historical Society
121 Hope Street
Providence, RI 02906
Telephone: 401-331-8575
Website: www.rihs.org

★ SOUTH CAROLINA

South Carolina Department of Archives and History
P.O. Box 11669
Columbia, SC 29211
Telephone: 803-896-6196
Website: www.state.sc.us/scdah

South Carolina State Library
1500 Senate Street
P.O. Box 11469
Columbia, SC 29211
Telephone: 803-734-8666
Website: www.state.sc.us/scsl

★ SOUTH DAKOTA

South Dakota State Archives
900 Governor's Drive
Pierre, SD 57501
Telephone: 605-773-3804

South Dakota State Historical Society
same address
Telephone: 605-773-3458
Website: www.state.sd.us/state/executive/deca/cultural/
    sdshs.htm

South Dakota State Library
800 Governor's Drive
Pierre, SD 57501
Telephone: 605-773-4950

★ TENNESSEE
Tennessee State Library and Archives
403 7th Avenue North
Nashville, TN 37243-0312
Telephone: 615-741-2451
Website: www.state.tn.us/sos/statelib/tslahome.htm

★ TEXAS
Texas State Library
Archives Division
1201 Brazos Street
P.O. Box 12927
Austin, TX 78711-2927
Telephone: 512-463-5460
Website: tsl.state.tx.us

★ UTAH
Utah State Historical Society
300 Rio Grande

Salt Lake City, UT 84101
Telephone: 801-533-3536
Website: www.history.utah.org

Utah State Archives
Research Center
Archives Building, State Capitol Hill
P.O. Box 141021
Salt Lake City, UT 84114-1021
Telephone: 801-538-3013
Website: www.archives.state.ut.us

★ VERMONT
Vermont General Services Center
Drawer 33
Montpelier, VT 05633-7601
Telephone: 802-828-3286

Vermont Historical Society
109 State Street
Montpelier, VT 05609-0901
Telephone: 802-828-2291
Website: www.state.vt.us/vhs

Vermont Department of Libraries
109 State Street
Montpelier, VT 05609-0901
Telephone: 802-828-3265

★ VIRGINIA
Library of Virginia
Archives Branch
800 East Broad Street
Richmond, VA 23219-8000
Telephone: 804-692-3500 or 804-692-3888
Website: www.lva.lib.va.us

Virginia Historical Society
428 North Boulevard
P.O. Box 7311
Richmond, VA 23221
Telephone: 804-358-4901
Website: www.vahistorical.org

★ WASHINGTON
Washington State Archives
1129 Washington Street SE
Olympia, WA 98504-0238
Telephone: 360-753-5485

Washington State Library
415 15th Avenue SW
Olympia, WA 98504-0238
Telephone: 360-753-5590

★ WEST VIRGINIA
West Virginia Department of Culture and History
Archives and History Division
The Cultural Center
1900 Kanawha Boulevard East
Charleston, WV 25305-0300

Telephone: 304-558-0230
Website: www.wvculture.org/history

★ WISCONSIN
State Historical Society of Wisconsin
Archives Division
816 State Street
Madison, WI 53706
Telephone: 608-264-6534
Website: www.shsw.wisc.edu

★ WYOMING
Wyoming State Archives
2301 Central Avenue
Cheyenne, WY 82002
Telephone: 307-777-7826
Website: http://spacr.state.wy.us/cr/archives

Wyoming State Library
2301 Capitol Avenue
Cheyenne, WY 82002
Telephone: 307-777-7281
Website: www-wsl.state.wy.us

INDEX